bonelight

Environmental Arts and Humanities Series

bonelight
mary sojourner

Ruin and Grace in the New Southwest

UNIVERSITY OF NEVADA PRESS ▲▲ RENO : LAS VEGAS

Environmental Arts and Humanities Series

Series Editor: Scott Slovic

University of Nevada Press, Reno, Nevada 89557 USA

Manufactured in the United States

of America

Design by Carrie House

Library of Congress Cataloging-in-Publication Data

Sojourner, Mary.

Bonelight : ruin and grace in the new Southwest /

Mary Sojourner.

p. cm. — (Environmental arts and humanities series)

ISBN 0-87417-510-0 (hardcover : alk. paper)

1. Sojourner, Mary. 2. Environmentalists—United

States—Biography. 3. Environmental protection—

Southwest, New. I. Title. II. Series.

GE56.S64 S64 2002

333.7'2'092—dc21   2002000069

The paper used in this book meets the requirements

of American National Standard for Information

Sciences—Permanence of Paper for Printed Library

Materials, ANSI Z39.48-1984. Binding materials

were selected for strength and durability.

FIRST PRINTING

11 10 09 08 07 06 05 04 03 02

5 4 3 2 1

For Lillie Anna Foltz,
for the woman missing on the road to Cadiz,
for the Beloved,
and for my Flagstaff neighbors who fought three years to protect
Dry Lake, the volcano wetland referred to in many of these essays,
and who won.

.   .   .

My gratitude for the losses that brought me
to these western lands,
for deep and abiding friendships,
for my editors, Sandy Crooms and Trudy McMurrin,
for my agent, Judith Riven, without whom . . . ,
for the Flagstaff Activist Network,
for a man who was once both cliff rose and mountain,
for the Once and Future Everett,
for those who have shown me the way,
and those who haven't.

.   .   .

For my grandfather William Foltz who opened his beautiful old
books to me and, when I was tired of reading, sat me in the heart
of his huge rolltop desk and put a pencil in my hand.

What I love about the red-rock wilderness is that it tells time differently. There's a sense of erosion and humility. This isn't real estate we're talking about. This is the body of the beloved.

—TERRY TEMPEST-WILLIAMS, *People*, 15 July 1996

Contents

Acknowledgments   xi

greenhorn

First Meeting   3
Opening   5
Connection   6
Greenhorn   8
Hunting   13
Spirit Level   14
Belly   18

stone egg

Watershed   29
Reclamation   32
She Changes Everything She Touches   34
Blood Moon   36
Stone Eggs   38
Shattered   41
White Piano   43
Lupine   45
Listen   47
Going Through   49

bonelight

Ragged   53
Ceremonies   55
You Could Say I'm Your Neighbor   58
Beautiful Weed   61
Bonelight   64
Real-Estate Porn   67
Running Out   70
Compromise: *Ghost Dance of the New West?*   72
Don't Tell   75
Portal Canyon   77

On the Street—2000 80

Super Downtown 83

Big Ditch 86

flip

Fire Ants 91

Flip 93

On and On 97

Coming Home 100

Buckskin 102

wild rose

Wild Rose 109

Desert Tortoise, Meet the Annihilator 114

Chasing Sevens 117

Bitch Bitch Bitch 120

grace

Grace 131

Guadalupe Project 133

November, 1997, Dear Jason 134

Mile Markers 137

Rank Stranger 140

Wild Heart 142

Monsoon 144

Controlled Burn 146

Stretch 147

Closing 149

afterknowledge

Outliving the Enemy 155

Outliving the Enemy—Again 157

the black work

The Black Work 163

Acknowledgments

The author gratefully thanks the following publications, in which some of the essays in this book first appeared:

Arizona Republic for "Greenhorn" (2000); *Brevity* for "Portal Canyon" (1999); *Flag Live!* for "Beautiful Weed" (1997), "Bone-light" (1997), "November, 1997, Dear Jason" (1997), "Wild Rose" (1997), and "You Could Say I'm Your Neighbor" (1997); *Flagstaff Tea Party* for "Outliving the Enemy—Again"; *Flagstaff Women's Newsletter* from 1990 to 1998 for "Blood Moon," "Coming Home," "Fire Ants," "Flip," "Going Through," "Guada-lupe Project," "Listen," "Lupine," "On and On," "Ragged," "Rank Stranger," "Reclamation," "Shattered," "She Changes Every-thing She Touches," "Stone Eggs," and "Watershed"; KNAU for "Hope"; National Public Radio for "Chasing Sevens" (1999), "Desert Tortoise, Meet the Annihilator" (1999), "Monsoon" (1999), and "White Piano" (2000); *Northern Lights* for "Bitch Bitch Bitch" (1999) and "Buckskin" (1996/97); *Sierra* for "Belly" (1993) and "Spirit Level" (1994); *Valley Guide* for "Buckskin" (1996/97); *Wildlands CPR Newsletter* for "Closing" (1998); *Writers on the Range* for "Big Ditch" (2000), "Don't Tell" (1998), "Mile Markers" (2001), "On the Street—2000" (2000), "Real-Estate Porn" (1999), and "Super Downtown" (2001).

greenhorn

First Meeting

Out here, light can be the raw calcium of old bone. Back there, in my hometown on the shores of a great eastern lake, light can be pewter or rose or burn like the heart of an emerald.

Out here, a Navajo meeting you for the first time might tell you the clans of her mother and father. Other times, a beefy guy in a beefier suv parks across the two handicap spaces outside the health-food store and, when you point out what he has done, says, "Who the hell are you?"

My mother's people were Pennsylvania-Dutch farmers. My father's people were Alsatian and so poor that rickets left him with bandy legs. Our town, Irondequoit, New York, was so small no one ever asked you who the hell you were.

When I was five, my parents moved to a two-bedroom apartment above a hardware store on a truck farm on the three-block main drag. I grew up weeding carrots, making velvety ladies from hollyhock blossoms, watching decapitated chickens flop in the barnyard dirt; learning to singe and pluck pin feathers, that you could eat the delicate shoots of milkweed, and that geese were the most terrifying animals on earth.

My father taught business, coached football, and sold real estate. My mother, at his bidding, stayed home, winter dark tugging the fragile neuronal tides of her brain until the sleeping pills the doctor prescribed seemed the only window to any light at all. She survived every suicide attempt she made. There were months in the state hospital, shock treatments, expensive psychiatrists, no health insurance, and my father working three jobs to make ends meet.

To be a depressed woman in the 1940s and 1950s was to be diagnosed as hysterical, narcissistic, manipulative. My mother believed the doctors. She rarely left our dark apartment. I was her only friend. Hard December light contained us, only the shimmer of our Christmas tree promising grace.

Then I held my first-grade reader in my hands. Words became sentences, sentences became story, and stories opened into infinite passages of light.

Three summers and three more suicide attempts later, my parents took us to a tiny Adirondack mountain lake, black water so clean we drank it, the aurora borealis silken above the northern shore. They showed me how to climb into the old canoe and balance. They tied a life jacket around me, put a paddle in my hands, and let me float along the shoreline. Alone.

Near twilight, I paddled toward the boulders beyond the point, away from the tiny light of my mother's cigarette burning in the long, slow dusk. I watched great brown bass drift below my paddle, turquoise dragonflies rest on my bare leg. August heat melted the scent from the pine. I waited for the first star, and when it pierced the east, I felt myself connected, as though a filament of light wove me into sky and water and the scent of the dark ragged trees.

That double light of story and connection has shone true— on the leveling and subdividing of the hills and creeks of my childhood home; on the gentrification of the neighborhoods we hippies rebuilt in the heart of an eastern city; and even now, on western towns and earth disappearing before our eyes, eaten by insatiable hungers as thoroughly as bone by cancer.

Under that light, in pure gratitude, I offer story and the possibility of connection, delicate and essential as desert bighorn bones in an unnamed Mojave wash—or as any first meeting.

Opening

To write about the New Southwest is to write about hunger and greed, emptiness and searing beauty. To write about the New Southwest is to be humbled again and again.

I write about hunger because I am perpetually hungry. I write about greed because I always want more. I write about emptiness because I, too often, feel empty, and that makes me kin to frantic developers, builders, hustlers, cardsharks, slot hogs—and billionaires, one of whom has said, "I am insatiable for land. I can't ever own enough."

I write about beauty because in doubting mine I have lost it, and I cannot bear to see the beauty of this western earth lost to bad faith.

I am humbled because I have limped into the throat of the Turtle Mountains, paddled on the San Juan River in the noon twilight of a solar eclipse, been swallowed and spit out by Rapid 24½ on the Colorado River, and stood helpless above an unnamed wetland valley watching bulldozers rip it apart.

I have changed the names of places and people in some of these essays for their protection.

Connection

As I gazed at the brown silt-choked waters absorbing a black plume of industrial and municipal sewage from Memphis . . . I experienced a palpable pain. . . .

I had no plans to swim in the river, no need to drink from it, no intention of buying real estate on its shores. My narrowly personal interests were not affected, and yet somehow I was personally injured. It occurred to me then, in a flash of self-discovery, that the river was part of me.

—J. BAIRD CALLICOTT, *Environmental Ethics*

And I am part of the river. I came here, to this desert light, these fierce and fragile streams and innately holy mountains, to learn just this. The lesson took nearly thirteen years and began the morning I stood in the shadowed wash behind Wukoki Ruin, asked for help, and promised my life to One-in-Whom-I-Did-Not-Believe. Help me feel connection with You. Help me feel connection with Earth. Help us protect You.

Slowly, so slowly that I doubted again and again, my prayers were answered, not only with moments of luminous joy on canyon rims, or rising up alive from Rapid 24½ of the mineral-green Colorado, or in the moment when I balanced at the top of a sandstone slab at Joshua Tree National Monument.

Those moments were gifts. I can never repay the givers. But the moment I knew I was part of earth and thus part of something greater than my small human life was the evening I looked down from a limestone ridge to a beloved meadow near my home, a meadow that is now a gated golf-course development a half-mile from a near-identical gated golf-course development, where for much of the year the golf course lies covered in snow, the mansions sit empty. I saw hacked-off stumps of ninety-year-old ponderosa pine and gouged ravines, blasted limestone outcroppings, bulldozed dirt blocking what had been a snowmelt stream, and I felt as though I had been ripped open.

Beyond pain, beyond anger, I went dead for one long summer. No human betrayal, no lost lover, nothing compared to the death-in-life in which I walked. I knew my heart had opened, my veins transfused with Earth's raw beauty, Earth's raw pain. I was grateful.

Months later, I walked up the hillside that looked down on the meadow. Despite the snow, it was easy, too easy. Bulldozer tracks cut down to mud and rock. I walked in them. You could say I was trespassing. You could say I was bearing witness.

Snow forgave the developers' work. Despite the electrical boxes and bright yellow hydrants, the earth looked much as it had a year earlier, dark pine trunks shining, a raven soloing in the winter-gray sky, last autumn's grasses gold calligraphy against the snow. I pretended nothing had happened. I turned my back on the bulldozed mud ruts and stepped out into the snow. I walked into what was left of the trees. I longed to turn back time, to have read the notice that would have told me this land was being sold and to have started fighting then. The raven, on cue, gave one mocking *scrawwwww*.

I remembered the Poet's Garden in the heart of the bleak northeastern city that was once my home. A mossy stone was set at the foot of an old linden. On it were carved the words "To live in the hearts of those who love us, is not to die."

In full-blown summer, I went back to the meadow. The workers were putting in roads, laying down crushed rock mined from some other ravaged place. They set up tasteful site markers, dark brown on green, in the woodsy script so beloved by those who take the forests hostage.

I stood at the edge of the road, wrote "No" in the crushed rock with a dead limb left from a ponderosa long ago cut and hauled away. I thanked the place, told it that I would be back till the gate went up and locked me out.

"My walking here will be your hospice," I whispered, "my heart, your grave marker; my writing, your revenge."

Greenhorn

The dog is the same colors as the leaves—she prances ahead, slowing only on the long hill that ends in the pine grove. The tips of the trees are melted gold in the late afternoon sun, the sky over the reservoir silver.

Later, leaving the frost-burned herb garden, I am halted by a ragged maple, blazing in last sun, incandescent as though lit from inside. I try to still my brain, to believe in miracles. What pours light on the dying tree?

—Journal, Rochester, New York, October 1980

Twenty long years ago, I had come to believe I knew too much, which was just enough to see through everything human and wonder why to stay alive. "What pours light on the dying tree?" began to echo in my unwilling heart, in the whisper of Stony Brook snowmelt over granite and the cries of Canada geese homing south over Letchworth Gorge, from a patch of wild violets in a trashed alley and young larch cones burning scarlet.

Now and then, I would see a print of the Virgin Mary in some bodega, standing on a black crescent moon, roses falling from her cloak, light flooding the boundaries of her body, her face the warm brown of Mexican *peloncillo*. "What pours the light?" I would whisper, and she would smile without a word.

It seemed a miracle my charred heart could hold anything. The city that my friends and I had reoccupied in the sixties, had rebuilt and reloved into vital beauty, had become a place in which we could no longer afford to live. Ramshackle houses and neighborhood diners, blues joints and secondhand stores, living-room food co-ops, the Free School, the beauty parlor where anybody could get their hair cornrowed, the coffee house run by Sicilians who'd come here in the thirties, the Ukrainian dry-goods store where you could buy beeswax and brilliant dyes to decorate Easter eggs, the bakery store that carried fresh cinnamon in wooden boxes—if they weren't bankrupt by the high rent imposed by new landlords, they had been bought by bright gorgeous people who raised the prices and painted the building San Francisco olive and mauve. Everywhere I looked, the death of what I had loved simpered back.

There was the death of a true friend, then of true love—and my own death, no longer sixty years away or fifty but zooming in closer with every morning I woke to gray weather, every hour I walked the city streets, watching my beloved home pimped to whomever had big bucks and the big *I want.* I poured gin down my throat, worked sixty-hour weeks, battled a fossilized health-care system with my clients, didn't write the stories I knew I had to, and tried to trust the question "What pours light on the dying tree?"

In 1982, my friend Ashley, a Cockney wild guy who loved the West so much that when he was a kid in London his mother gulled him into eating liver by telling him it was buffalo, popped the question that changed my life. One ice-bound 2 A.M., as we sat nursing my gin and his eighth beer, he said, "This summer, let's go out west. You'll love it."

"Thanks, but no thanks," I said. "I've been there. Too boring, too beige, and too big."

"Just the Grand Canyon," he said.

"The Grand Canyon is Disneyland with rocks."

"I bet you fifty bucks you're dead wrong." He clinked his glass on mine.

Six months later, we took off. On an Indiana six-lane, I looked around at miles of malls. "I hate the West. I want to go to Maine."

"Fifty bucks riding on this," my pal said, "and Indianapolis isn't the West."

In Colorado, St. Mary's Glacier melted slower than time into a crack in my heart I hadn't known existed. A mountain dream later, my friend walked me, eyes closed, to the edge of Grandview Point of the Grand Canyon.

"Open your eyes," he said gently.

I did. In a heart-jolt of vast aurora rock, I was taken. Amazed. Knowing I knew nothing, and nothing was exactly enough.

December 28, 1984, I drove west, Ash riding shotgun, my Firebird hauling a trailer crammed with what could not be left behind. We both pretended Ash was there because he loved the road. We both knew I was terrified. Still, with tears flooding my eyes, I insisted on driving away from my home and grown kids with the steering wheel in *my* hands.

"Are you sure, luv," Ash said, clutching the dashboard, "that you don't want me to drive?"

"Forget it," I whimpered and headed south for the throughway. In the instant the front wheels of the Firebird touched down on the road, my tears stopped. I raised both fists in the air and howled, Ashley grabbed the wheel, and the first part of my life was over.

I felt as though I was launching into pure space. I had packed economy-size toothpaste, twenty pounds of good linguine, quarts of olive oil, a five-pound chunk of Parmesan cheese, and ten bags of Bokar coffee. When an eastern friend asked, "But how will I call you?" I said, "On the phone."

"But what if you're not there?"

"The phone machine will take the message."

"What phone machine?" she asked.

"The one in my house."

She threw back her head in laughter and said ruefully, "I keep picturing you in a tepee in the middle of the burning-hot desert, and I couldn't figure out where there would be an electrical socket."

I smiled wisely and didn't tell her about the toothpaste and the Parmesan.

I drove into Flagstaff, Arizona, on January 4, 1985, ten days before my forty-fifth birthday. I'd been lured by more than the Grand Canyon. Here were the long, sweet lines of the San Francisco Peaks; the scent of ponderosa pine; the proximity of fierce blue desert shadows; and—by Ed Abbey's definition—a lifetime of good works to be done.

Twenty minutes into town, I called the gas company. I expected the usual three-day wait.

"What are you doing right now?" the guy said.

"Eating breakfast at Choi's."

"How long'll that take you?"

"I don't know. Half an hour, maybe less."

"Meet me in forty-five minutes at the house," he said. "We'll get you all fixed up."

I went back to my *huevos rancheros*. Ashley looked up from his steak and eggs. "How'd it go?"

"Ash," I said, "I love this place."

My fourth full day Out West, I drove Ashley to the Phoenix airport, climbed back in the car alone, and headed north. Night began to move in, a quarter moon dropping toward the Bradshaw Mountains, whose name I knew only because every fifteen minutes I pulled over and studied my map. I wondered why the moon was in the west when I knew it rose in the east. I wondered why the saguaro had faded away and what was the name of the low shrubby tree whose scent seemed greener than green. I wondered how I would write when I knew the words for nothing.

Heart in my throat, I pulled off the Interstate at Montezuma Well, bumped onto a dirt road, and kept going. The highway lights faded. There was no one on the road. I wondered if I should have brought water, if my bones would one day be found. I turned off my headlights and slowed the car.

The world went lilac, then a color I had seen only in the hearts of opals. A black shape paused at the edge of the sand, and I slammed on the brakes. A barrel-bellied wild pig minced across the road without so much as a turn of its head. Later, I would go to a Sierra Club meeting and announce that I had actually seen a javelina, *j* as in *java*. A woman would grin. "That's *havelina*," she would say, and I, who had always needed to know everything, would grin unashamedly back.

This morning, autumn moving in, soft rain hissing outside my cabin, I remember "*j*-avelina," and hiking all of the Devil's Garden Trail at Arches National Monument in April with no water, and sleeping for the first time outdoors, on a picnic table in the campground, wondering about scorpions and rattlesnakes and losing that wonder in the wonder of Orion and, later, in a midnight blizzard of stars.

I remember taking the Firebird in for its first Arizona license and the inspector walking around the car, saying, "Looks pretty good to me."

"The left directional light is out," I said, my Catholic girlhood training running my mouth.

"Honey," she said, "you must be a greenhorn. Out here, we think that if God had wanted us to have directionals, He wouldn't have given us a left arm."

"I *am* a greenhorn," I said. "I've been here six months."

"Stick around," she said, and patted my left arm. "You won't be green for long."

She was wrong.

Though a statue of the Mary I now know as the *Virgen de Guadalupe* now stands in the southwest corner of my living room, roses spilling from her cloak, her bare feet planted firmly on a black crescent moon; and I know that juniper sometimes smells more green than green and other times like wildcat piss; and I have been arrested for trying to stop a uranium mine on sacred land and will probably be arrested again, I am still a greenhorn.

When you ask, "What pours light on the dying tree?" you are willing to be a greenhorn—and when you are happy to never have an answer, you are a greenhorn forever. Curious. Foolish. Small and surrendered. Eternally in love.

Your beloved is beautiful beyond anything you have ever known. You are willing to be astonished and clumsy. As you go out to meet your darling, you are afraid.

You move, in imperfect grace and not knowing, as a woman might set her greenhorn foot on a trail over Cima Dome, see it disappear in a tangle of Joshua trees, going impossibly out and away, toward an ocean of sky, into absolute mystery—and she begins walking.

Hunting

The trail moves through a high desert meadow. I am walking. I am hunting the glint of last light off obsidian. I carry a fossil found at a curve in the trail, a pale sandy pebble fluted with ripples. I hold not so much an ancient sea creature as time. What I hunt is not so much stone as light. This is the magic of where I live. I reach out toward something, and what I am given is time, light—and searching the color of the southern clouds: globe mallow, fire agate, a hawk's glowing tail feathers.

Spirit Level

What my father wanted to give me was not mine to take. What I wanted was not his to give. More than anything, he wanted me to return to the northeastern home and the old religion in which I was raised, and to find a good husband. What I came to in 1985—high desert mountains, dark pine and amethyst light, alpenglow, white water and cedar smoke—are temple and lover enough.

This is where I breathe, where I balance, where I live. It is one of a thousand, a hundred thousand, places, some yet unknown, where, if I stop, I look, listen, and touch. I have no doubts.

What I wanted from my father was that he would know this. He would visit. We would row an old wooden boat on a twilight-still lake where we would fish till darkness melted around us and when we cast, we cast into mountain stars. The black shoreline, the silent sky, and he and I would hold a peace I had felt when he rowed our family out onto the evening mirror of a little Adirondack mountain lake. We would float on this opal western water and I would tell him that he had taught me to find peace in wildness. He would smile, and what had nagged between us would finally be still.

"Rocks," is what my father really said. "There's nothing out there but goddamn rocks. Why would you want to go all that way just to see a few rocks?"

In April 1992, after six months of harsh and persistent wasting, he went much further. My brother called at 1 A.M. "He's gone," he said, "peacefully. One of the last things he said to the doctor was, did it seem to be time to get a handicapped sticker for the car?"

We laughed.

"Will you be coming for the service?" my brother asked.

"No," I said. "He and I talked about it. He said there was no point in coming all that way once he was gone."

"I don't understand," my brother said, "but it's okay."

I lit a Guadalupe candle and set it on the porch. My dad had loved that Great Mother. Orion, distant diamond brother, moved across the black sky. A breeze came up carrying the scent of ponderosa. Somewhere, I swear, I heard a great horned owl, one cry, only that, no answer. It seemed strange to me, and comfortable, sitting on my porch, wrapped in my sleeping bag, my father's death brand-new in my heart, all held in the cool quiet off the mountains, as though my heart was cupped in a giant, stony hand. And of course, it was not enough.

A year later, I drove back east. Alone. What I needed to do could not be done in the company of anyone. My father was dead, my mother in an extended-care facility. There was a river I needed to revisit, a greater river to cross, new shapes of stone and water and light to find. That much I knew. The rest, the journey to the human places, that was beyond mapping. There was no trail guide, no Trip-Tik. Only silence held the way.

I drove without music on an Oklahoma two-lane bordered with flame-orange gaillardia and olive sage, below thunderheads that never broke. I camped on the banks of a dammed river and watched mist luminous as pearls rise into evening. Boats and RVs and people became the ghosts on a Japanese scroll. Fireflies moved in and out of the fog. I dipped my hand in the cold water, breathed in mist, and tasted river.

Next morning, deep in a limestone cave, I closed my eyes and listened to a wild rivulet pour over stone. I set my palm flat against water caught in travertine pools. I promised the cave owners I would send them postcards of the blue-green falls and bone-white travertine at Supai.

I drove on, over a rolling state road just above the southern Missouri border. I found the little river town that I remembered and a dirt road that curved down into green light. There, in air that smells like life itself, you can hike north along the eastern bank, and when you are ready, you move out into breast-high water. You lie back, and you are carried. Now and then you look up to mark your way. When you rest your head on the water, you hear pebbles clicking along the bottom. I thought of the Colorado, of how it had closed over me two years earlier and held me, and I had been so afraid, and I whispered to the bright southern sky, "Thank you."

There was a Witch in that place, and later down the road, across the greater river, a Christian. We talked about prayer and we laughed about balance, these two women and I. Somewhere in between, I looked in my rearview mirror and saw smoke from a burning field rise across a bloodred sun. White birds, and black ones that might have been cormorants, flew away from the fire. A dull-blue iron bridge rose in front of me, pewter water stretched out below. The Mississippi held me for an instant between my western home and my birthland to the east. Breath rose in my throat, and I was across.

I stayed alone in my parents' house. My father was fully gone, my mother still present in her cooking tools, her embroidery and books and the pot of molding homemade fudge sauce on the stove. I cleaned the fridge, did the dishes, thinking how she would laugh when I told her—I, the little girl who raced outdoors right after dinner, away from the soapsuds and chores out into the mysterious summer grasses, into the emerald then violet light. When all the dishes were gleaming in the rack, I walked out to her roses. I knew what was there. She had told me. "He's in the roses."

I was bathed in the warm twilight of my childhood, in a town on a Great Lake's shoreline, on the banks of a broad river, on hilly land covered with subdivisions and roads and shopping malls, no longer shining with creeks and ponds. I looked down. There, in the black earth at the base of those impossibly green bushes, luminous as the salmon roses catching the last light, were the chips and shadows of my father's bones. I didn't touch them. I waited till the light was gone. Then I walked down into the basement.

It was cool there, and dark. I thought of caves, of rivers, of minerals carried down and washed away. My father's tools hung neatly on their pegs. I had never touched them. I took two old screwdrivers with worn wooden handles. Something overhead caught the light. I reached up. It was his spirit level, stained and dusty and, when I set it on his homemade workbench, still true. I looked down at the tiny bubble catching light in fluid as green as a winter southwest river. Later, I would go to the garage and find his ax. I would know what I needed to do, to take it home to the mountains, to juniper, aspen, and pine. Ax and spirit level, work and prayer. And all those goddamn rocks.

Now, a month later, the spirit level sits above my southern window. In the West, at this time of day, they are blowing up old ammunition at the abandoned army base. To the north, the San Francisco Peaks hold wildflowers and prayer feathers and traces of last spring's snow. East, beyond my front door, the road moves out, through dry gaillardia rattling in the wind, past little rivers that run above the earth and below, curving by burned fields that sprout next fall's harvest, across that great gray water that has taken back acres of Her own, near the homes of Missouri witches and Tennessee Christian women, past talk of balance and prayer.

In the center of my western cabin, I take down the spirit level. I tilt it east and west. I think of rock and water and green light, and I am grateful that what brings me back to balance is just that.

Belly

The first time I saw the place—the giant pines, the squat and fragrant juniper, the countless grasses and low bushes, flowers that seemed to be a dozen different shades of purple, birds, tracks, the earth and stones beneath my feet—I knew the names of none of them. I was two months in this high desert country. I had read Ed Abbey and, from twenty-two hundred miles away, in a city where the names of trees were elder, oak, and maple, the flowers rose and tulip and geranium, the birds starling and robin, the earth buried beneath asphalt and concrete and perfectly groomed lawns, I had longed for this space, tree after tree, warm red and gray glitter underfoot, light and beauty I could not name. Standing at the edge of that old-growth meadow, in Arizona late-winter sun, I had no idea that by the time I learned the names, and the name of the place itself, the place would be gone.

The north and south rims of the Grand Canyon of the Colorado River hold some of the richest and most accessible deposits of uranium in North America. The name of the geological phenomenon that contains the ore is breccia pipe. To mine uranium from breccia pipe, you sink a shaft, drill, and haul. You need equipment and buildings, holding ponds and berms, access and haul-out roads; you need, somewhere, a mill; and you need to know that for $150 a year in maintenance and investment, under the 1872 Mining Law, you can hold claim to that land, that breccia pipe, and all the wealth that lies inside it.

You need to believe that forests are for multiuse management and that the name of the place can be written on a claim, on documents in your lawyers' offices, on your income-tax return, on statements of profit and loss. You need to believe that the name can be written anywhere but in the heart. Your North Rim mines are named Hack and Pigeon, Hermit and Pinenut. You begin exploratory drilling thirteen miles south of the South Rim of the Grand Canyon, and you call the place

Canyon Mine (Proposed). You do this quietly, in the name of keeping things easy. You do it, you say, in the name of wise use.

Long ago, long, long ago, there was a Grandmother. She had two grandsons. As boys will do, they set out on their adventures. This Grandmother tied threads to the doorway of her house . . . it was one of those houses made from bent saplings and rushes put over them . . . and she waited a long time. Those boys were gone a long, long time. One day, the Grandmother looked at the threads and they were dripping blood. She became very sad and she tried to kill herself by stuffing dirt down her throat. It did not work. She lived.

This all happened up there by Red Butte, up about a mile or two from where those Denver people want to put that mine. There is more. . . .

The next time I saw the place, I'd heard it was named Canyon Mine (Proposed). I had gone to meetings in Flagstaff and heard the mining company engineer, a loud, jolly guy with an abundant gut, flannel shirt, and worn Levi's, tell us that when they did the exploratory drilling, they hadn't seen no animals, hardly none at all. You could tell he'd misnamed most of us, hippies and eco-freaks and old-timers alike, as one after another, with relatively good grammar, we stood up and told him and the Forest Service honchos what we thought of their plan.

We named our objections. We used terms like *rape* and *annihilation, old-growth meadow* and *permanent habitat destruction.* We said that no matter what you named it—the proposed leveling of 13.7 acres of National Forest land and the improvement of miles of Forest Service roads and ten years of ore hauling to the mill in Blanding—whether you named it wise use by a mining company known for its mitigation efforts or taking what's rightfully yours by law, an Environmental Impact Statement (EIS) was required.

The engineer called us names. We responded. And, somewhere far north of the shouting, the place was silent. There was a fat three-quarter moon. Snow fell on the thick dark branches of the trees, light shimmered off the snow. Maybe a raven cried out. Maybe a coyote trotted across the fresh snow, chased a mouse, caught it—only the tracks remained.

The following weekend, a few of us, who shall be unnamed, drove up the main canyon highway, turned off on a Forest Service road, and barreled through snowmelt and gumbo mud to the edge of the place. We looked toward the center, to the bare earth, the exploratory drill-rig, the bulldozer, and we named what had lived there: ponderosa pine, Utah juniper, Gambel oak, cliff rose, four-winged saltbush, buckbrush, buffalo berry, pale wolfberry, rabbit brush, Mormon tea, banana yucca, big sagebrush—the sage that grows where the earth has been disturbed, soft, pale leaves that we crushed between our fingers, whose scent we breathed in deeply, knowing that we found it where trees and juniper had been chained. Out loud, slowly, our voices quiet, we said, "Hill lupine, Palmer lupine, verbena, penstemon, and fleabane, locoweed, and wood betony."

"Steller's jay," we said. "Raven, wild turkey, black bear, antelope, deer and elk and coyote, mountain lion, bobcat, red-tail hawk and eagle, worm and lizard and ant."

One of us, a tall man bent with arthritis, knelt and touched the ground.

"Kaibab limestone and shale," he said. "Toroweap sandstone, Coconino pure quartz sandstone, quartzite, slate, and schist."

We turned and looked off into the untouched forest. Snowmelt ran clear, ran away from the place, away to the south, away to the north, toward Havasu Canyon, toward the home of the Havasupai, toward the blue-green waters that fed every moment of their lives; it seeped in, down through earth and rock into the Muav-Redwall aquifer, that great subterranean stream system, so vast and complex it has never been charted. At our feet, where the earth lay bare except for bulldozer tracks, the water ran metallic orange and yellow. We thought about holding ponds and hundred-year rains, about something trickling down, drop after drop, trace upon trace, monsoon after monsoon, year after year. The tall man stood.

"Let's go," he said.

We'd come prepared. Banners and prayer feathers, Gods'-eyes, wooden stakes and bright ribbon, blue and green and purple.

"Canyon Mine," we hollered, "we take back this place!" We went to work. We staked it out, all 13.7 acres, north to south, east to west, feathers shimmering in the late-afternoon light, ribbons flying, stakes pounded deep into the earth. Someone hung the banner across the drill-rig. "Place," it said, "claimed for nothing human."

Well, the two boys had all these adventures, some of them pretty good, some of them pretty bad. They met some girls, and one of those girls got a baby from one of those boys. That was down there by our canyon, down by the blue-green water, where the reeds grow. You know that place.

All the meantime, that Grandmother is up there in those trees up by Red Butte, and she is missing her boys and she is crying. They had ways of knowing things back then. We forget them . . . most of the time.

The Environmental Impact Statement (EIS) took a year. When all the letters and claims and counterclaims were almost over, the Havasupai People, the tiny, five-hundred-member tribe whose name means People of the Blue-Green Water, stepped forward. They said they had information for the Forest Service. They said they had waited because they would have to tell things they weren't supposed to tell. When the EIS was released, the Forest Service anthropologist wrote that the Havasupai had no discernible religion and no claim on religious rights to the land. The Havasupai said that they had not trusted the man and so they had told him nothing. They said that to hear what they would say, to hear the name they would give that place—the exact site of the mine—you would have to be prepared, you would have to move through ceremony. They said that to do otherwise would risk a great deal, for them, maybe for everyone.

Those were some bad times back then. There were bad people. The boys got killed in a way I can't tell you. But the girl raised up that baby, that was the grandson of the Grandmother, and one day he went back to find his Grandma, you know how kids are. That trip there was so long. . . . I think he went on a horse . . . that he was a grown man by the time he got there. Up there near Red Butte, where they want to put that mine, up where our old people still pick those medicine plants . . . up there. . . .

The head ranger went through all the stories and statistics. My unnamed friends and I visited the meadow. We saw the toppled corpse of the big juniper, the head-high piles of dead sage and wildflowers. Now and then, an unmarked truck drove in and waited while we hiked the perimeter of the place, while we sat in what was left of the grasses, near piles of limestone and quartzite and slate, ate our lunches—and watched the light change, and the weather, and the way the wind moved in what was left of the trees. We might even have pissed on something metal and bladed, something almost as big as the downed juniper.

We drove the proposed haul route, took photos of elk and turkey, the narrow shoulders on the highway east from Grand Canyon National Park to Cameron, the narrow bridge over the Little Colorado, the washes that carved up the Navajo Reservation, that ran back to farms and ranches and homes, the signs that said Flash Flood Area every few miles along the road. My friend drove and I spoke into a tape recorder. I described sand the color of pink pearls and clouds like veils and rock like, like . . .

"Hell," I said to my friend, "Ed was right. This rock isn't like anything. It's not a cathedral or a courthouse or an amphitheater. It's not named Kayenta Sandstone or Navajo. It's not stubborn as memory or fragile as hope. Its name isn't even rock. What it is, just is. I give up."

We made a slide show and dragged it from little town to big city. I wrote. Others sang. The EIS process dragged on. I got to know some of the Havasupai. They got to know us. We learned each other's names. They learned that we held the place holy; we learned that all they wanted was to get this over and go home. One late-September weekend, we gathered in the big sage-filled meadow below Red Butte, a few miles from the mine site, and we talked and ate and sang and danced and told stories. Some of us called it prayer.

So this boy who was now pretty much a man, finally gets back to where his Grandma lives. He didn't see her, though. Her house was there, but she was gone. He waited around awhile. Maybe it got cold and the flowers died and there was going to be snow. Still, he stuck around. Kids had respect for their Grandmas in those days.

One day, wintertime, he saw something. It was his Grandma and she was riding a horse. He got on his horse and they met right there, up near Red Butte, up near where they want to put that mine.

The head ranger decided that the mine and the miles of haul route through the ponderosa pine and juniper and elk and snowmelt *would have no significant impact.* The Havasupai and a few of the environmental groups appealed his decision. Eight of us closed a road in the park. We put on white radiation suits and linked hands. People sang. Kids carried banners. Don't Nuke the Canyon, they read, and Save the Sacred Land, they read, and Honor Grandmother Canyon, they read.

The media came and told us that if we wanted them to cover our next demo, we'd need to destroy property, get hurt, something exciting like that. They shot a few pictures and left. Security took us away. They cuffed us and drove us back to Flagstaff, past the road that leads into the mine site. It was a bright November day. The sage was soft and green. Afterward, we—you can read the names in some eco-rad newspaper story somewhere—agreed that if you had to get busted, up there, up thirteen miles north of Red Butte, near where they want to put that mine, that was the place to do it.

So, the Grandson and the Grandma, they met up there on their horses and they were happy to see each other. Every year since then, on that same day, they do that. I can't tell you exactly how, because it's a secret, but how they meet up there in that place where they want to put that mine, up near Red Butte, that's how our religion goes forward. That's how it lives.

Because up there, right where they want to put that mine . . . that's where the Belly of the Mama is. She births out our religion, and the boy and the Grandma help it go forward. If they stick that mineshaft in the Mama's Belly, well, you can see how that would be. Our friend here, Clark Jack, he told the Forest Service how it was. "It means, a robin, when it lays its eggs, if you go touch its eggs, the mama won't come no more. . . . That is what is meant by destroying our sacred site. It couldn't be no more. There will be no more."

I go up to that place, that place that could be named the Belly of the Mama, a few times a year. Now, there is a ten-foot-high chain-link fence around the bare earth. There is a headframe and holding pond, equipment shed, maybe a Cat or a backhoe. When I arrive, I ring a buzzer, and sometimes a guard comes out and I tell him that I'm there to pray. Other times, two fuzzy dogs barrel out toward me. The lead dog snarls a few times; the rear pup, whose left eye is blue and whose right eye is brown, holds back. I offer a muffin or what's left of a burger, and both dogs chow down. They whine with pleasure. I remember all the times I've prayed up here—the women's circle on winter solstice, the four Havasupai gatherings, once a year around about autumn equinox, and, a few miles down the road at Red Butte, the fiftieth birthday when my unnamed friends and I brought up a tape deck and played Tibetan Buddhist healing chants to the place, and then a little Aretha Franklin singing "R-E-S-P-E-C-T."

I walk away from the gate toward the forest. Maybe I tie a raven feather to a tree limb; maybe I just sit on the red earth and tell it all the letters we've written, the meetings we've held, the phone calls we've made. I tell the earth that uranium prices have dropped and that the company has closed its North Rim mines and put Canyon Mine (Proposed) on hold. I tell the earth that I know She's lonely for the Havasupai bones and artifacts that the salvage archeologist dug up and shipped south. I tell Her I hope that all of it is safe somewhere, hidden in some dark room underground, away from curious eyes. "The bones of our ancestors," a Havasupai elder told me. "We can only pray for them." I look up into the brilliant sunlight, then back to the bare red earth.

"Belly of the Mama," I whisper. "I will never forget your name."

stone egg

Watershed

1994 TRAVEL NOTES: *The forthright emptiness of southeastern Oregon, Lake Abert, stinking to high heaven and populated as heaven might be, with Canada geese, avocets, and the fattest ravens I've ever seen; three hours, seventy miles an hour on 395, in all that long way, I see six other vehicles; the plain friendliness of people in the country's scuffling towns—all of this like peroxide on an infected place.*

Two days earlier, I had driven along the coast of the Olympic Peninsula, across Whidbey Island, and into Seattle. When I stepped out of the truck in an obscenely expensive parking lot in Pioneer Square, the world spun.

"I think this is the big one," I said to my friend. "I'm having a stroke."

I've been a hypochondriac since I was seven. She knows me.

"I don't think so," she said. "Every time we get within five miles of a town on this trip, you hyperventilate."

Breathing in fast and hard, as an animal does when under attack, adrenaline a laser in the blood. Nowhere to run, baby, nowhere to hide. Can't not see what's around me—charm, clear-cuts, five lanes of bumper-to-bumper traffic, families with five kids, six, seven; espresso kiosks in every shopping center. What's in my face are small towns, once part of a living web, now cloned into a thousand-mile shopping mall that stretches from San Francisco to Eureka to Portland to Seattle and, perhaps, in my worst nightmare, strangles the globe in a noose of twelve-bucks-a-pound coffee beans, gourmet ice cream, genuine Native American dream-catchers, enviro-cosmetics, T-shirts and baseball caps, Hilfiger, Hilfiger, Hilfiger.

I crossed the fierce watershed of the Sierras a week earlier to meet my friend. She is fifty-four, as am I. We weren't sure why we were taking five days to drive up the Coast, and what we discovered was harder, more beautiful and terrifying than either of us could have imagined. She—but that is her story, her awakening. I learned how much the last nine years in

Northern Arizona have ruined me for modern life. I learned that I need very little. I learned that I could, in hour after hour of terror, keep driving, keep seeing, keep breathing, keep bearing witness to what I felt and what I saw. I learned that the towns I loved were the ones left shabby, and that a clear-cut slashes your heart, no matter when you see it, but wounds most deeply as you drive your truck past black sand beaches, fierce gray water, and rain forests so green they hurt your eyes.

I learned that loggers are terrified for their livings, a few of us are terrified for the trees, and that too much of the rest of the world—poets and professors and lawyers and delightful people walking the boutique row of Pioneer Square in Seattle, Washington—may not care.

Watersheds lie everywhere. On one side lies passion, on the other the rain-shadow desert of denial, of the illusion that you can be safe. Ironically, it was in the wet emerald country that no one seemed to care, and the rain-shadow desert held places like the Yakima Tribal Museum, where Chief Owni reminds us that "in time immemorial, the Creator made us of this Mother Earth and placed us here," and where Spilyay the Trickster challenges us to "live harmoniously with nature in all forms and moods."

My friend and I crossed, as we have so often, the watersheds of our friendship, from young women to middle-aged, and now to aging. Part of what we learned was this: she, tall and slender and blonde, a woman who has turned heads for thirty years, and I, stocky and dark, were both invisible. Somewhere on the Washington Coast, on a black beach where white stones were moons upon the earth, we looked at each other, we said it out loud, "We *are* invisible." And we laughed.

She remembered I had written that women who saw themselves through men's eyes would disappear. We said we were grateful to see each other, and to see what needed our witness. We walked up the beach and wondered who made the connections between big profits and clear-cuts, between infinite

constellations of corpo-espresso neon and housing developments spreading across the western earth. We promised each
other we would make the connections visible. My words. Her
paintings. Our witness pouring down from harsh watersheds.
East and West.

Reclamation

Sweet dawn softened by the possibility of rain. I wake to heat rising in my body. I uncoil from the sheets, let the breeze move over me, old fire within like fear or anger or passion, early-morning air gentle on my skin. I try to remember the last time I bled and can't.

I cup my breasts in my hands. They are slack. Never, after breast-feeding four children, were they the breasts of a fourteen-year-old, not since I was twenty. I love their weight in my hands.

This is a small revolution, feeling terrified and proud and furious and powerless over how my long time on this earth moves in my cells. Last night I read about female-to-male transsexuals: one of the guys said, "Testosterone really heats the system up," and I thought about hot flashes. I thought about the balance of hormones, how we are nothing but ocean, tides moving in us, and how, just when I most love being a woman, the balance may tilt toward male, or neuter.

I pull on a sweatshirt, go to the porch, and write:

I don't want to be neutral or faux-male because my body chemistry is shifting. Chemistry is a lovely word. I imagine brain-tides following the moon, coral pools holding salt water, memories, dreams.

What lives in those shining puddles cannot breathe out of water. I am water. What lives in me breathes what I breathe. Summer air. Sage smoke. Tobacco. Exhaust. Pine scent. My chemistry responds. I go where I can breathe. Now, time slipping quick as salmon away from me, it matters very much. Where I can breathe. Where I can speak. Where I can live my age.

When the heat floods, when I flood myself with heat, I love living this change. One of the infinite gifts of my work is that I can dress in soft, loose clothes. So the heat rises like a sweat, a sauna, and I remember how, long ago, my relations and I crawled into a cave in some Alsatian mountain range. We closed off the entrance, heated rocks, piled them in a pit, poured on water, perhaps scattered herbs. In the dark, in the pure steam, we crouched over ourselves. We slowed our breath, we were silent, we sang. We felt that which was no longer useful melt from our blood, our muscle, our bone.

Later, standing naked under ice-indigo sky, listening to the stars, we thanked wood, fire, air, water, and black rock. We thanked each other. Out of the singing emptiness inside each of us, we thanked what moved us. We thanked what held us still.

Perhaps a year ago, on the shore of a spring-swollen desert river, a woman who was no longer my friend tilted up her beer and said, "I don't want to get old." She looked at my lover, she looked at me. "I don't want my breasts to sag. I don't want to shrivel up." My lover looked carefully past her.

Sister, I would say if we were still speaking, *what you fear is moving toward you. Should you be lucky enough to age, your breasts will sag, your skin will wither. You will feel heat rise up in your body. You will be invisible to men. You will be with nothing but your own fear and courage and joy.* If she heard me, she would think I spoke a curse. When you hear me, when you see what shines in my eyes, what moves in my aging body, my leaping spirit, across the pages of what I write, you know it is a blessing.

She Changes Everything She Touches

This evening, Orion sequined against a black sky, I walked to the water house, drew hot water for my dishes, and walked back. My breath shone in front of me, vaporous as the clouds that wreathed the mountains I could no longer see but knew were there, rising up against night, hanging over the holiday glitter of my home. The gray cat ran beside me, stepping into the powder snow, raising her delicate paws and shaking them, crying out to me to move more quickly, more quickly. Silver and shadow filled the world.

I poured hot water over my dishes. Steam rose, clean and sweet. I picked up the first cup and set it in the suds. Lisa Thiel's *Songs of Transformation* spun into the room. She sang of goddesses and cascades and stars. A porcelain Kuan-yin and an ivory-colored hare stood on the windowsill. A gray big-breasted clay rabbit rose three feet tall on the counter, Swedish geranium twining around its belly. On the altar to the east, Ixchel, the Mayan moon goddess of the healing arts and childbirth, embraced her springtime consort, the Hare. There are a hundred rabbits in my cabin, fifty Ladies, more moons than I can count. Our Asian sisters, at least the ones who remember, see a rabbit in the moon. I have seen the moon, mysterious silver in a big hare's eyes.

I rinsed the cup. It rested in the drainer, steaming in the cool air. Behind me, the wood stove turned wood to warmth. I remembered hating to wash dishes—when I washed them for seven, when only I washed the dishes in which only I had cooked the food only I had bought, the dishes in which only I had served the food only I had grown.

Now, washing dishes is pure beauty. This cup is mine. This coffee stain. This crumb of baked potato. This rice. This sauce. This sliver of apple skin, translucent as the moon. These dishes, none matching, each a gift, drying in the cabin's deepening warmth. The water, four gallons, which will cool and be poured on the Swedish geranium, the avocado, the peony my friend Chris gave me.

The music ends. I rinse the wash pan, hang the cloth to dry. The fire leaps in the stove. Earlier, I sat here with a friend. She sat with tears. She sat with what she believed was nothing, which was her living alone. We sat in silence. There was nothing to say. Nothing gave way to tears. Tears to nothing. Nothing to peace. Nothing to nothing. We sat and the juniper burned and the stove gave off heat.

She changes everything she touches . . . everything She touches changes . . . She changes everything she touches . . . everything She touches changes . . .

Blood Moon

What you call your period, we call our moon.

October '93: Full moon rises above black pine. I love Her. She is my sister.

When the moon that glows in me rises late, I miss Her. *Is this the beginning?* I think. *The end?*

When She floods my thighs, I smile. I step out onto dry pine needles, under the rising moon's bloodred light, I give Her back to earth. I look down, and up, and down again. I follow Her where she leads.

August '94: She goes ragged, month by month, moon by moon. I go blind, feeling my way in darkness, in silence, along pure heart line. I mark my calendar, and the design makes no sense—and all sense.

January '96: She is gone, no longer a scarlet talon, a wild cat's eye, a red feather of light that rises, floats, grows more and more vaporous till it cannot be seen, and returns, a sliver of garnet, a pomegranate seed, a sweet river in my flesh, gone, returned, gone. Thirteen moons ago, I crouched over pure snow, bleeding, and for the last time watched Her puddle round and red as the October moon.

Now, She is pure shadow. Reflecting nothing. Heat rises in me, and fear.

My mother told me these days would come. Moonless. Calmer. No more pain. No more mess. Wildness tamed. Fire damped. Darkness a blessing. I did not believe my mother's reassurance. I do not now.

I am without season. Without light. I imagine circling under black pine, in pure dark, searching, not knowing what I will find.

December '96: My back gives out and I go flat. There is nowhere to run if I could. I read till words blur. Friends visit. I am grateful when they leave. I check the calendar. Two years ago, I bled on snow.

I try to think of obsidian moons, of onyx, try to name my loss with beauty. I want a goddess, a ritual, something precious to hold against my empty belly. There is nothing. I am alone. The moon in my belly is dark. I am aging and, sure as my life, some-day I *will* die.

I fly toward that cold fire. I drop into that knowledge as thoughtless as a moth and am consumed. Not moving, I move beyond the speed of moonlight, into places where the sky goes black, candles gutter and die, the dark rises up, thick and soft as good cloth. I wrap it around me. I cannot breathe. And can.

I move, not moving, from the hollow in my belly, following breath, past black pine, toward black stars, in an obsidian sky. I go toward the black rock circling our earth, and I remember that the moon we cannot see is called the New.

Stone Eggs

For my friend, artist Barbara Fox, on her fifty-seventh birthday

For long gray-green days, the monsoons circle these mountains. I water sunflowers and poppies, feed corn chips to ravens who are blue-black as the clouds. I stand in the heart of the meadow. Purple lupine and penstemon, purple cranesbill geranium, its sepals yolk yellow, blossom at my feet. I raise my fists to the wild withholding sky, and I say, "Rain, damn you, rain."

I give up and come inside, where I circle around a hard story about two women growing old. The inevitable. Alchemy. Eggs turned to women, women turned to stone, eggs turned to stone—one malachite, river-green veined with cloud; the other polished opal, city lights glittering in its center. My fear and my intention weave a nest around them, a nest of strands pulled from the human heart.

I remember when we first met. You wore a long, clingy dress, pale sand, the same color as your hair. I think the material might have had metallic flecks, but that is more my style than yours. I don't know what I wore, black most likely, something short so that men's eyes would be drawn to my legs. Your lover had just said to me, a perfect stranger, "I'd like to pour brandy on you and lick it off." I'd turned, looked at his flint eyes, and said, "You're nuts. That would burn."

A minute later, you appeared. And from then on, he was little but a shadow.

That was twenty years ago, twenty-five—I think now that we were made of desire. Ten years later, we were mothers sexier than our daughters, makers who darted, too often, into the arms of anything but our craft. I came to your new house, a place in which you lived alone. I remember a nest and two stone eggs. I don't know if I have made this up, one gray marble egg, a second that might have been tumbled from turquoise, perfect for a house that was the lair of an elegant magpie.

And my nest? A raven's. A dusty mishmash of good paintings by unknown painters, cat hair, rainbows and daggers, feathers and geodes and bones. If we tried to live together, one of us would shortly be mad or dead.

Apart twenty years, twenty-five, still friends, still the sisters neither of us had—you painting, not-painting, married, mothering, grandmothering, your nest in the heart of a city; me, writing, not-writing, alone, e-mail the link to my sons and daughter, my nest in the heart of pines and growing devastation.

You break eggs, smear them on canvas.

One quartz egg sits at the center of my writing altar, a gift from an editor. I light a candle. The egg shimmers, its shell golden, its heart opal. I think of you hours and miles away, standing in your studio, puzzling, aching, one egg in your long fingers.

Throw it . . .

. . . as I come to this shimmering screen. Afraid. Angry. For days, this story runs ragged in my blood. "Stone eggs," I have muttered. "Forget it." To write the words "stone eggs" is to write my body, to slowly fill the page with a woman hopelessly beyond beauty, a woman whose legs might draw men's eyes but whose face they will not see. Stone eggs. And, worse than invisibility, my desire petrified, my body withered and dry. I can bear not to be wanted, but not to want is a death-in-life.

I walk to the mailbox, away from this page, and I think of us on our last road trip, edgy, irritable, our hearts breaking in joy on black beaches, in green rain-forest light, on roads too hard to drive, too beautiful not to. I remember the rock shop south of Eureka, how we both wandered the aisles of amethyst and carnelian, stony wood and Apache's tears, shelves filled with eons, and the glittering instant when a geode is cracked open. We held slices of stone to light. Saw secrets, saw the heart of the earth glowing like late-October sun.

The mail holds no rejections, no excitements. The sky complicates itself. Light goes silver, clouds marbled with the promise of rain. *Stone eggs*, I think.

Geodes. Thunder eggs.

I know the last words of this story, and I walk back home.

We are geodes, my friend and I. What lies inside emerges only in the breaking, beautiful as mystery, stubborn as love.

Shattered

My time splintered, my sight, my speech and hearing, on this soft May noon, when my mom is dying two thousand miles east of here. I am in pieces because this woman I have both hated and loved is leaving and I am slowly coming off a brief attempt to take an antidepressant that was not right for me and tomorrow I will climb on a plane flying east to be with my dying mom, my brother, daughter, granddaughter, the son who lives in Hong Kong, and the son who lives in Japan—and I am terrified. Next to going crazy from this medicine, the thing I fear most is flying, the thread that holds me to the holy mountains stretched thin, thinner, perhaps beyond holding.

I may not see my mother, my friend Lillie Anna Foltz Mammosser, again. She is going, perhaps gone, the eighty-five-year-old woman who hobbled into my brother's office wearing a slouch hat and the shades she had to wear because of cataract surgery, looking, my brother tells me, "like a really scary Blues Brother." She leaned on her cane, tugged the hat over her forehead, and said, "Hey, Billy-boy, da boss wants to see youse."

That woman is gone. And the woman sitting naked in the bathtub and I, four, thought her breasts looked like hot-fudge sundaes, and fifty-one years later I looked at her tiny shape in the big nursing-home bed and told her that story. I helped her change out of her vomit-stained sweater and saw her withered, nearly sexless body, more osha root than woman, more woman than what you see glittering on M-TV. She looked down at herself, grinned, and said, "My breasts aren't what they used to be." That woman is gone.

The woman who decorated our house at Christmas with pine and candles and light, teaching me about ceremony, about holding back the dark, weaving in the thread that led me to my present life, my home in the pines, the candle burning in the Guadalupe holder for the woman dying in the East. The woman whose last words to me may have been *Blessed be.*

And much, much more. The woman who taught me to taste

everything, who looked at me on those last moments of conscious contact and said, "I overfed you," and I laughed because I love my big body and *she* taught me to take pleasure with food. She made Austrian Wind Torte piled high with buttercream roses; chow mein when everybody else in the neighborhood ate meat and potatoes; steamed clams with lemon butter; curry and beef Stroganoff and sweetbreads and the best Pennsylvania-Dutch chicken-corn soup you ever ate.

My mother's beauty could go on forever. And will. Grief could go on forever, for her forty years or more of relentless terror and depression. Gratitude seems sweeter because, a few years ago, she told me that the goodness of her years from seventy to eighty-two made up for all the pain that had gone before.

I give thanks for shopping trips downtown, Sibley's Christmas maze and seven-layer cake and lying to my dad about how much my new loafers cost. Thanks for that which is always holy: the power of words and music, the sacrament of beauty, Billie Holliday, Marian Anderson, the last long note played by some unknown jazz pianist in some unknown dive.

On that last conscious visit, I asked her if she wanted to talk about dying. She smiled. "Oh, yes. I want to talk about my legacy to you and your brother." She paused. "Nuttiness and the piano, and . . . laughter. Not just ordinary laughter, but the kind where tears run down your cheeks."

"And you wet your pants," I said.

"Absolutely," she said, and closed her eyes. Again that smile. "That's it," she whispered, "nuttiness, and the piano, you know what that means, jazz and gospel and Bach, and laughing so hard tears run down your cheeks and you wet your pants. That's it. That's what I want to leave you."

"So be it," I said. "And blessed be."

"Blessed be, dear heart," she said, and for a while she slept, her smile never fading.

White Piano

My mother, in her deepest heart, was a jazz pianist. She had perfect pitch, could learn by ear anything she heard on her cherished records. "Satin Doll." "Don't Get Around Much Anymore." Oscar Peterson. Marian McPartland. "The best by the best," she'd tell me.

She made music every day, but I never heard her describe herself as a musician. My mother played only in the living room of our home in small-town Irondequoit, New York, most often to an audience of no one. Or to me, who couldn't stay on key if her life depended on it. My father was a man of his time and did not want my mother working outside the home. She came to believe that it was better that way.

I'm way outside the home. I've brought my notebook to the open cocktail lounge overlooking the Reno Hilton Casino gambling floor. It's 10 A.M. I left the breakfast buffet, ready either to gamble or to write. The little cocktail tables and big soft chairs made my decision.

I open my notebook and hear piano music. A shiny white baby grand sits on the veranda just above me. The piano bench is empty, and the piano is playing under a chandelier made of gold birds and purple globes that my mother would have found atrocious.

The piano begins to play "Misty," Errol Garner's classic. My mother's favorite song. I go to the empty bench and sit next to the invisible pianist. I watch the keys move, remember my mother's small, sure hands, a cigarette burning perpetually in the ashtray next to her. Morning or evening, bright sun or shadow, she always wore dark glasses. Back then, all that was missing was a blue spotlight.

A tall young woman walks by, pauses, and looks at my hands folded in my lap. She grins, "You play very well."

"Thank you," I say. "'Misty' was my mother's favorite song. She died five years ago."

The woman nods. My tears are easy, an old knot in my heart loosening. "My mother," I say, "was a jazz pianist."

"Wow," the woman says, "lucky you." She walks away into the slot glitter and jangle.

The piano plays on. I consider putting my hands on the keys and don't. That was *her* gift. The words and the empty pages in my notebook are mine.

Lupine

For so it must be, and help me do my part.

—*Tibetan prayer*

I sit on my bed, in this small cabin at the edge of a meadow filled with dry and jade grasses, sun dazzle and shadow, purple lupine and vetch. There are more purple wildflowers per acre in this part of the country than anywhere else. A botanist told me that. She spread her arms wide and laughed. "And here we are."

We looked up at the purple mountains. Around my feet, glittering limestone caught the light. We were not imagining any of this. Where I live, in the middle of my life, in the middle of this place, each day is full of magic. I've taken firm hold of my own trembling hand and walked myself back into the center of flowers and mountain and light.

I'm afraid a lot. This business of surrender, this business of defying every lesson of my 1940s girlhood, of sitting on this bed, speaking to my dead father, "Whether you like it or not, I grieve for you; whether you like it or not, I'm crying." This business is my work.

Lupine sustains me. Chopping firewood sustains me. Carrying water. Dumping ashes from the fire.

Light and shadow drift in toward the edges of emptiness I have opened, the great space where once dumb hope lived. Sometimes I walk under the Sacred Peaks with only that lonely freedom. Sometimes I sit in circles with women, with women and men, and what shines between us is just that loneliness, that freedom. In that, we are not alone. Sometimes I keep a promise and, in that, make amends. Sometimes I make amends and, in that, keep a promise.

These words are for my friends and kin. They are for any of you who walk this hard and healing path. By circumstance. By gift. In reluctance and by choice. This path moves in and out of light, under sun, moon, stars, past lupine, through pine, into canyons and up mountains. It races through cities and curves through high desert. It spirals down. Only you know what lies there. It spirals up and carries us, all of us who are lucky. And stubborn. And brave.

May we meet here. On this path. For so it must be, and help me do my part.

Listen

What do you hear? Listening when you did not expect to, what do you hear? The highway whines a mile from my cabin. Jays and ravens *scrrrrkkkk* in this bright air. Fiona, the gray cat, mewls at my ear, purrs against my cheek, leaps to the desk. Pens, books, and scissors clatter to the floor.

What do we hear? Outside ourselves, pouring through the open window, singing in the night air. Whining, unwanted, from the contrail above our homes, our canyons and rivers; from the streets outside our doors, the dirt-bike trails, the bulldozers shaping hills and wetlands into money.

The world outside speaks to me, roars, hums—even its silence falls on my ears, enters, is part of me. The world inside says more. My back says, *Slow down, slow down, stop, be gentle, think about me, honor me, let me be your prayer.* My brain says, *So much to do, autumn spins in, wood to carry, firebrick to set in place, pinecones to gather in scented piles . . . so much beauty to see, the last wild-red penstemon and how sunset falls across them, a feather on the path and how it catches light, chestnut mare loping across the meadow, brown against gold, how she suddenly wheels and races, running toward who knows what . . .* and I walk, this bright autumn, slow as a great blue heron, less graceful, flight nothing more than a dream.

The world inside speaking: Kali, Morgaine, Pan, bear, raven and rabbit, Crone and tiny child, all of them speaking, each voice growing louder, ringing in my heart, quieting, fading, gone quiet, whispering, howling again, dawn to dusk, in my dreams, in the tides between my wakings, awake.

Ride the bright edge, they say. *Snuggle safe in your cabin, quiet as an acorn in its shell; make vengeance, make amends, dance as though you were bright silk on the wind, be wind moving through bright silk.*

And more, hesitant, insistent:

Listen, attend. I am your aging. I am the moon-pulled tides of womanhood, ebbing, flowing, ebbing, flwing, the sea diminishing, growing more salty, less sweet, the moon upon its surface more seen than felt, its light fully as bright, gleaming.

I sit on the edge of a slickrock point a little north of Muley Point. Hundreds of feet below, the San Juan River coils through gray walls. In this dying September light, the water is bronze. The far horizon burns scarlet. Small pools in the rock are silver. The wind rises, and waves move across them, and they are mirrors of motion and twilight. I cry softly. Love seems to be all around, holding me in radiance, rock, and silence, in glowing red sand and piñon, juniper, ephedra, and sage. For a moment, what chatters inside is quiet.

Thank you, I say. As though echoes bounce from light, rock and silence, I hear voices from within: *Claire is my name, and Angel. I am Delicate Arch and the sixteenth floor of a welfare hotel in a city frozen in winter terror. I am your dying father. I am the guy who sat in a one-room cabin near Dolores, Colorado, and held off his father-in-law with a P-38, and I am the old man who told the story. I am the woman in black cotton who told you how to rip and tie T-shirts to make them look cool, and her voice trembled and her fingernails rattled on the arms of her chair, and she had done so much speed she hadn't slept for days. I am this light that washes over everything, and dies. I am that star, that one, there.*

I lie under everything. Bedrock. Molten. The heart of it all.

I am the stories you have yet to tell.

Listen.

Going Through

I drive my old truck to the base of the obsidian flow—two miles of black glass one hundred feet high. The road is a two-track, weaving over red-brown ponderosa duff, past clusters of purple lupine, a wild black-water creek, through the delicate light and shadow of a Sierra near twilight.

I stop, climb out of the truck, and am, as always, edgy. I am a woman, fifty-nine. My lower spine is damaged. No more backpacking. No more solo river runs. I will never be alone in the places I love best without being afraid. Not as long as I can reach them. A road, insistent as fear, will always cut through the beauty.

I leave the keys in the ignition, the driver's door open, and set up my one-burner stove and plastic camp chair. The western light begins to go molten. I heat the leftover soup from lunch in Bishop and break sheepherder's bread in chunks, my back to the obsidian flow, my gaze flicking from the bread to the dirt road. I am ready, at a heart's jolt, to jump in the truck and drive away from soup, bread, stove, chair, from obsidian flow, sunset, and the solitude in which the world is most luminous.

The horizon burns rose-gold, the obsidian flow is a dead-black serpent against the fierce light. I turn my chair to face the sunset. I eat in uneasy peace. Light fades, goes salmon, shell pink, seawater blue. The forest is, in an instant, dark.

Abruptly, the rock serpent dazzles, crevices and outcroppings dusted with diamond light. Near-full moon ices the obsidian, glitters on boulders the color and size of big-city Cadillacs.

I study the forest behind me, no lights, no distant engine whine. I raise my eyes to the dazzling rock, the delicate sky. I watch till long after midnight, alone, joyful in the presence of my most faithful companions. Fear. And wild beauty.

bonelight

Ragged

Two nights ago, I walked out the dirt road to find the forest around the seven-trunked ponderosa pine devastated. They had cut every small and medium tree. I cursed them, those who did it, those who ordered it, those who believed you can fix the unfixable.

This morning, Everett and I and our new friend, Baker, are in Everett's kitchen. A few minutes ago, we came back from a visit to the seven-trunked tree. Since yesterday, they had gone back, cut one of its trunks, the one we called the gatekeeper. I sat down in the desolation, set my hand on the raw stump. Everett was quiet. Baker explained about cutting the forest for its own good. I knew he was right and I didn't care. He tucked a pinecone in a pine knot, and I set it on the stump.

The seven-trunked tree had six trunks aligned in a circle open to the east—and a seventh, the gatekeeper, to the north. I once thought of the circle of pine as She. These days I no longer think of trees or rocks or places as He or She. These days, I am sick of human attribution.

The seven-trunked tree stretched up in a ragged circle. Pine needles lay thick and fragrant in its heart. Birds lived in its branches—Steller's jays and doves and sparrows.

You could sit in the heart. Alone. With a friend, a lover, a friend become a lover. Mostly, I sat alone. I gave small things to the trees. Glittering rocks. A lump of pine resin. A dead raven. Four jay feathers. Water. The pine needles rained down on my offerings. Something dragged the raven away. Now, you would never know I had given anything. As it should be.

The seven trees contained my joy. My tears. My rage. When I wrote, when love came to me, when I returned safe from journeys, when, suddenly, I wanted nothing, had only light, air, and pine in perfect beauty, I sat in the circle, turned my gaze to the east, and said, "Thank you." In the last four years of death and loss, I bowed my head to the pine needles, the stony earth beneath me, and said, "Help me." I longed for a lover to hold me, to cradle me in his arms as the pine cradled him. There was no lover, so I leaned back against the western trunk and was truly held.

As luxury golf-course gated housing developments metastasized in our forests, as Newt Gingrich came to Flagstaff, held a melon in his hands at the Northern Arizona Food Bank, said that volunteerism deals better with hungry families than "bloated government bureaucracy," and then attended a one-thousand-dollars-a-plate fundraiser for J. D. Hayworth, anti-family Republican legislator, in an undisclosed location in a gated development, I took my rage to the pine circle. I wrapped my arms around the big trunk to the north and prayed for wisdom.

Six trees and one to guard the gateway. It was perfect. And now, six trees. I will walk out tonight. I don't know what I will find. Six trees or none.

Today a local columnist tried to link the need to thin the forests with a justification for more commercial cutting. The papers's editorial, defending expensive real-estate development, said, "If you could build 20 homes costing $100,000 and make $3,000 profit on each, or you could build twenty homes costing $200,000 and make $6,000 profit on each, which would you build?"

I thought about writing a letter: "Some of us would not build at all." Instead, I wrote this, ragged as a circle of six trees and a stump. And in a few hours, when pure light and air and pine are more than enough, I will walk out. I will touch the remaining trees. I will say, as I do so often these days, "I am sorry."

Ceremonies

There are rumors. They drift on the hot hard wind.

This was a strange November, bright and balmy, grasses pale gold, stubborn bindweed blossoms starring the cinder pile near the shower-house. And now the rumors. I wondered if what drifted was true.

We were in the climbing gym. "This drought?" T. said. "Did you hear? About Spirits visiting the Rez?"

I pulled on my climbing harness, shielded my eyes against the sun glaring through the big window. I felt shaken. Not by his words, but by the wind, the thirsty air, by my own long drought.

"So?" I said. I trust him. He's just innocent enough, and cynical.

"A Navajo woman heard someone at her door. When she opened it, two Spirits were there. They told her about this drought. What needs to be done. The woman got afraid, ran into another room; her daughter talked with them. Something about four ceremonies. The Navajos know only two of them. I guess there have been calls on the radio for elders, for somebody who knows the Old Ways."

I bent to tie my shoes. I was glad he couldn't see my face. I was swept by sorrow. The Old Ways. My people's Old Ways. Where?

"I wonder what we can do," T. murmured.

No one said anything. I was surrounded by friends, and there was nothing to say.

"Maybe the Hopis—" I stopped.

My climbing partner moved out of a stretch. "Hey." He looked into my eyes. *I know what you're feeling.* No words were necessary. Our silence was not a drought. "Let's climb."

A few days later, clouds moved in. I went to Macy's Café for preclimbing caffeine. Shayne reached out and hugged me. "I went climbing yesterday. It was *great!*"

"Where? I thought the forest was closed because of the drought."

"Jack's Canyon," he said. "Oh, Mary, actually, you would have been so pissed."

"What?" I used to hike there. I remember perfect shadowed limestone. Perfect light. Perfect monkey flower and penstemon, and not-of-this-earth creatures pecked in the rock.

"It's bolted," Shayne said. "Everywhere. Cracks my fourteen-year-old kid brother could place protection in. Jesus, all these Day-Glo jocks with a rack full of quick-draws swarming over the rock like—"

"Maggots," I said. "Let's go cut bolts," I said. I didn't even know what I was talking about, but I know that when I see metal in rock my belly aches.

"Shit," he said, "they'll just drill 'em in again."

I think about ceremonies. I wonder if the best ceremony is no ceremony. Buy less, want less, take less; give away, reuse, pass things on. I wonder about a new clan: the Clan of Enough-Is-Enough. I wonder what our totem animal would be, and I realize that any wild thing would do.

I read Chuck Bowden's *Blood Orchid*: "Imagine the problem is that we cannot imagine a future where we possess less but are more. Imagine the problem is a future that terrifies us because we lost our machines, but gain our feet and our pounding hearts." Imagine a ceremony, I think, for which there are no expensive altar cloths, no crystals, no doodads or gewgaws, no chalices or cauldrons, nothing but what is present.

Outside the climbing gym, monsoon clouds hung gray as Inca doves. Troy looked out the open door. "Here it is."

Kath and I unhitched, went out. A few raindrops fell on my arms and face. We stood on the gravel, faces upturned. Kath and I spoke to the rain. I raised my arms to the sky, as always. We were very old just then, all of us. I knew this: weather is weather, a weave of air and temperature and water complex beyond my longing, a weave of elements not fickle or punishing or merciful, elements precisely as uncontrollable as the hydraulics of the Colorado. As random a blessing as passion.

"Thank you," I said. The rain stopped.

I climbed a long time, walked Buffalo Park, breathed in faint rain-scent, let it be enough. I wondered if the Navajos had found the old people. I wondered if the Old Ways were coming to the light. I decided to begin a series of invitations to ceremony. Poems. On telephone poles.

This is not fiction, I would call it, and I wondered if anyone would respond. I decided to send the words to friends in other cities. *This is not fiction. Come to the ceremony. I do not know where it is. Perhaps everywhere.*

I drove home the usual way. And it was not usual. Someone had altered a sign near the new luxury condos going up south of town. What had once read "The Pines at Woodland Village" said this: "The Pines *Are Dead,* The Pines *Gone Forever.*" I grinned and drove home.

A few days later, the sign was gone. A few days later, it began to rain again. Not a lot, not enough, but a beginning.

You Could Say I'm Your Neighbor

Opal midsummer twilight, I camped on the Gros Ventre River in a little BLM mom-and-pop campground. I talked with Anne, a seventy-three-year-old woman who travels with her seventy-five-year-old husband in an old Airstream Trailer, loving her freedom and terrified of the day her handyman-mechanic husband dies. I told her that my best friend, Everett, and I had been on the road for ten days, driving through northeastern California, southeastern Oregon, southern Idaho, southwestern Wyoming, looking for a place not being homogenized. Everywhere, million-dollar houses pocked the hills. Everywhere, mom-and-pop businesses went broke while Starbucks and Wal-Mart and Century 21 bloated bigger. Except in the small Mormon towns of southern Idaho, the locals all said, "The folks who work here can't afford to live here. Where do rich people get all that money?"

"There's nowhere left to go," I said to Anne.

"That's right," she said. "George and I have been looking for what we call 'our utopia' for ten years. It just gets worse. These rich people move in, push up the real-estate prices, hang around a few years, get bored, and move on. Then these little towns are ruined." She fixed me with a raptor's glare.

"Don't you run," she said. "Stay where you are. Hold your ground. You have to fight for what you love. In the long run, that's what counts."

Everett and I are home. All summer, I have watched development eat Flagstaff, a zillion new subdivisions out Lake Mary Road, up Route 180. Of course, there is Forest Highlands "The Meadows" gouging the shape of a beloved valley until it makes me dizzy to try to find the contours I once knew so well. I have held despair at bay by thinking I could find a haven—somewhere. Anne's words jolted me out of fantasy, and I found myself feeling not hope but the willingness to fight.

Everett and I staple an old bed sheet to a pole. We crouch in the early-autumn light in the back meadow, writing "Development Kills the West" on our banner. We stand in front of the barren site for the new Cineplex multimovie theater near Woodlands Village.

"Woodlands Pillage," I think. I wear a black band tied around my right arm. I am extraordinarily happy to be standing here holding our banner in the company of my friend. In the course of an hour, thirty people honk and give us a thumb's up. Two guys throw us the finger. I wonder if only the few making money from development want it, and about how they keep winning. One out of fifteen—you'd think those odds would mean something.

A man approaches us. His size, his age, what he wears are irrelevant. These days, developers wear hiking boots and faded jeans. They tell you, as this guy does, that they really respect what you're doing, hey, hell, don't get them wrong—they *love* the trees.

At first, this guy doesn't speak. He steps out on the median and takes our picture. "Smile pretty," he says.

"I'm happy to tell you my name," I say. I reach out my right hand. He shakes it. He does not say his name.

"Where you from?" Everett asks. The guy is startled. He pauses.

"Uh, for right now, from here," he says. "Yeah, you could say I'm your neighbor. You know, I've fought for more than a few trees in my life, too. Besides, this is just scrub woods, no big deal."

We nod. He goes on. Silence is sometimes the best subversion. By the time he's finished talking, we know he owns the business that is building the Cineplex. He retired once, but now he and the wife get to go all over the country to places they've always wanted to see, a lot of cute little towns. Hey, he just does his job; it's the rich guys on the city councils that let these things happen.

He and the wife go into a beautiful place, he does the job, they stay five or six months, then move on. Why, he's got sites all over the country. Just doing his job. If he doesn't do it, somebody else will.

We listen.

"You know," he says, "you're doing this too late. You should have been out here before this got started. You should of protested to the city council."

"Thanks for the advice," we say. I remember years ago when Wal-Mart wanted to build here in unbroken forest and some of us fought it and were told, "Just this one development, nothing else."

"God bless," he says, and he is gone.

Later, a sign goes up and we see his name. He's from Cucamonga, California. "Scrub woods, no big deal," he said. Nothing but young ponderosa and limestone boulders luminous with lichen and, in spring, tiny flowers starring the forest floor. Scrub woods, like they don't have in Los Angeles, on whose outskirts Rancho Cucamonga lies.

Everett and I will continue. Please join us. Or, like the young photographer who stopped and documented our work, take ten minutes and tell us how you feel. Honk. Give us a thumbs up. And later, pick your own position. And hold it.

In the long run.

Beautiful Weed

A yellow flower grows on the slopes around Dry Lake. The flower is called *beautiful weed* by the Navajo, and if you place it where you sleep, it will keep away bad dreams. Dry Lake, this soft September morning, is not dry. The lake bed is wet green. The aspen ringing the place have yet to turn silvery-gold. We stand on the wildflower-dotted slope, and we imagine how this will all be a month from now, when the aspen shimmer and the sky is fierce October blue. We imagine two years from now, maybe less, barred by security guards from standing in this place and, were we allowed in, seeing only another executive golf course, lodge, condos, and $750,000 houses in which people live a few weeks out of the year.

"It's a bad dream," I say to my companion. "And we're going to need more than *beautiful weed.*"

Dry Lake, at the end of Flagstaff Ranch Road, is proposed for development by a local subdivider and developer, the Flagstaff Ranch Golf Club (FRGC). The corporation recently bought the land, which was used for fifty years by the Zanzucchi family as a dairy ranch. Hikers, mountain-bikers, people drawn to meadow and basalt outcroppings, aspen, and aster have for decades, as my companion and I did this morning, "trespassed in beauty." Should the FRGC gain permission to develop Dry Lake, only those able to afford property in the range of $500,000–$1,000,000-plus will have access.

The $500,000–$1,000,000-plus price range is my guesstimate, because when I called the FRGC for information I was told, "We're a long, long way from determining what prices we will assign, but in the range of Forest Highlands." Who can afford $500,000 for a homesite, $1,000,000-plus for a house that he will occupy only a few weeks out of the year? I think of the huge, ghostly houses sitting unoccupied in the luxury developments, of security guards riding golf carts on asphalt roads through a cemetery for the living dead; and I consider what once lived in the place of these outrageously expensive trophies—not even so much the creatures, the lupine and wild morning glory, the great blue heron and wood ducks—but undisturbed rock and light, silence, the beat of a raven's wing, the delicate web of interdependence between lichen and rock and beetle. If we do not stop unbridled up-scale development soon, we are in peril of living in the heart of a giant gated mausoleum.

My companion and I stroll illegally along the northern edge of Dry Lake. She stops, picks up a piece of chert. "This has been worked. Have they done an archeological assessment here?" I tell her that an environmental assessment firm wrote that no archeological survey had been conducted within the project area and that no obvious prehistoric remains were found during wildlife and vegetation surveys. "Really?" She bent and picked up another stone. "Well, this one has been worked, too. I bet if we walked this place, we'd find more than artifacts. I bet we'd find sites."

All of this is enough for me. During my talk with the FRGC, the developer asked me how long I had been in Flagstaff. "Twelve years," I said. He laughed, but there was no warmth in the sound. "Well, I guess you're a newcomer. The wife and I have been coming up here since 1940."

"I believe," I said, and I was not laughing, "that I have lived in such a way that I have a much longer history with this place." I didn't go into details. I had already told him that we came from absolutely different beliefs about land. I told him I had a deadline to meet.

"Wait," he said. "Just one thing. You used to meditate in that State Trust Land meadow that Forest Highlands is now developing, right?"

"Prayed."

"Were you aware that you were trespassing and that it was illegal? The only way you could legally be there was if you bought it. Surely you respect legal property rights."

"Legal," I said, "is not necessarily right."

I promised to call him, and I will.

I suspect that when we talk, he will tell me that this new proposal follows a 1982 proposal that was approved by the county and that this proposal is good because it is lower density and has fewer commercial impacts. He will point out that the Forest Highlands Golf Course that destroyed part of Griffiths Spring Canyon was named a prizewinning environmental golf course. He will talk about loving the earth and private-property rights and how profit incentive is what this country is built on.

I will go home to the four sprigs of *beautiful weed* that I gathered today and dried in a clay pot near my desk. I will set them near my bed, and I will remember picking them, walking around the bush, telling it I would use the flowers only for medicine, thanking the plant, the earth, the sun, and the rain. When I prepare for sleep, I will pray for Dry Lake to be kept free from bad dreams.

And I will do more.

FOOTNOTE: I called a meeting in a local park. A dozen people met in the rain under an old, old cottonwood. That was the beginning of Friends of Dry Lake and three years of relentless work. In early winter of 2000, papers were signed that protect the volcano crater and wetland absolutely.

Bonelight

The developer wants to talk. "People with different viewpoints owe each other the courtesy of listening." I look out the back window of my cabin at the meadow, at *Mirabilis* blooming amethyst in the tall grasses, at the houses of the old suburb across the field. *Viewpoints.*

We agree to meet at a local restaurant. I hang up and call my friend Baker. "I don't know," I say. "Time is precious. This guy and I don't have common ground."

"You never know," Baker says. "We may be able to touch his heart. I want to try."

The day before the lunch meeting, the developer calls. "How about we meet at the clubhouse at the golf course? That's the only way my wife can join us." In ten years, I have never been allowed into the gated second-home "community." Once, not realizing that the forest was walled off, I drove in, hoping to see what lay on the other side of the huge culvert that slashes across Griffiths Spring Canyon, and found myself barred from entry by a nice young man in a nice little gatehouse.

"Okay," I say to the developer. "Do I need a pass to enter?"

He laughs. "Don't worry. I'll call the gate, and they'll let you in."

Baker doesn't like the change in plans. We talk about clans, about our suspicion that there are now two on this earth and that the distance between them is growing. "I'll go," he says. "It's the only way we'll ever get in there."

The clubhouse chandelier is made of antlers. I suspect if I mention it, this bone light that I've seen in every wannabe woodsy condominium and restaurant in the Nouveau West, I'll be told that the antlers were found discarded on the forest floor, and any other questions I have will be countered with assurance that this place, this big, pseudoclassy building and the impeccably groomed land on which it sits, is the last word in ecologically sound planning.

The developer has brought his wife and his environmental

consultant. Baker, I, and Third Musketeer Everett, down from trail maintenance in the Wind River Mountains, take our places at the table. A basket of fake pansies lies between the two clans. Baker orders a salad. Ev and I have already eaten. I will not let the developer buy me food. I wonder if the prohibition against eating with the enemy is as old as the DNA shining in my cells, as old as being willing to call someone "enemy."

I sip water and look past the developer toward the alien green of the golf course. I wonder what once lived here, in a vibrant messy web of life, death, and resurrection. The developer and I consider each other.

"What I want to know," I say, "is how creating these places feeds your soul."

He raises his glass. I think I see his hand shake, though it could be a trick of the bone light. "First," he says, "how much of what I say will be public? You already quoted our other conversation."

"That's true," I say. "You would be wise to say only that which you know will be repeated."

"Okay," he says. "Then, I believe we are all here for a purpose to serve one another and that the good Lord gave us this earth to use wisely."

The woman working as our waitress brings Baker his salad. The pale chunks of meat look like processed chicken. I think of the developers' plans for Dry Lake and the description of housing as "condominium-style product." Product salad in a product room under product light, looking out on a wild place become product.

Our meal, our talk lurch on. The developer refers to the earth as a "little blue marble." His consultant talks about mitigation: "After we nuke the place," he says, "we mitigate above and beyond what we've done." He uses the word *nuke* a lot. He's honest—hey, development is inevitable; somebody's got to do it. And he and the developer believe that they are doing the most environmentally sensitive job possible. Nuking the place and mitigating. I listen. I nod. I owe them the courtesy.

I think of Dry Lake. I remember Griffiths Spring Canyon, limestone, cress, and elk track braiding themselves into a living thread you follow to the huge culvert through which you glimpse the dead chemical green of the golf course, and I see the earth as a woman. She has been beaten and raped. She is not dead. The psychiatrists ask sensitive questions. They decide She is depressed, not essentially, but as a consequence of near-deadly abuse. They prescribe medication. She resumes a life. *Nuked and mitigated.*

We are told that the gated community into which we have been briefly welcomed is wonderful for family closeness. "Golf is great. A boy can be out there with his dad, doing what Dad does." The developer tells us he feels honored to provide a beautiful place where people from "down south" (Phoenix) can "recreate."

I ask him why he wants to develop more expensive home-sites when houses costing $200,000 are not selling. "The average resident of Flagstaff," he says, "can't afford a $200,000 home. My end of the market is for people who live elsewhere and can afford property in the half-million-dollar range for recreation. This is America. They have that right."

It's time to go. "One thing," I say. "You keep referring to the earth as a little blue marble. I don't agree. The earth is a web. Everything is connected. And the earth is not here for our use, wise or otherwise. We are temporary. We are stewards."

Baker, Ev, and I climb into Baker's truck. "Hey," he says, "we'll probably never get in here again. Let's drive around and see what's to see."

We head away from the clubhouse, across the culvert from which you can look down on autumn wildness to the west and seasonless clipped green to the east, back into a necropolis of elegant, empty second homes, and out onto a road that runs between the golf course and Highway 89A. Bailey curses. He stops the truck.

"This," he says and points to a tiny clump of cattails at the side of the golf-course road, "is what's left of Linbergh Spring." We climb out. "Right here," he says, "under this asphalt."

Real-Estate Porn

This isn't real estate we're talking about. This is the body of the beloved.
How can we not take a stand?

—TERRY TEMPEST-WILLIAMS, *People*, 15 July 1996

I'm not making this up. I wish I were, the glossy brochure that arrived in the mail today, complete with shots of the San Francisco Peaks, snow-dusted, of course; kitschy southwestern interiors loaded with kachina dolls and bogus artifacts; what might be Chaco Canyon masonry; and a close-up of the heartwood of a downed ponderosa. The development lies on what was once Museum of Northern Arizona (MNA) land and is rumored to be a result of the MNA's finances hitting shaky times—in part, one might conjecture, because the museum's potential benefactors are using their wealth to acquire ten-thousand-square-foot trophy homes and exorbitant golf-club memberships rather than support cultural resources in their mountain playpen. Witness the financial failure of our local Center for the Arts and the delicate balance between ruin and survival maintained by many of our local arts organizations.

Here is part of the text of this real-estate pitch:

> Does your life journey road map point to [blah-blah-blah buzzword] Springs . . . ? It Does! If you want to live in a boldly original new community where the earth and the mountains and the art of indigenous peoples will pour into you so you can live what you believe while immersed in nature to feel the awe and beauty of wild flowers, coyotes, elk, mountains, Ponderosa pine, and you help mold and craft a new house of wood and stone where you will join a mythical but real community made from the dreams and desires of all those others living on a homesite amidst forty-three acres of forest in the heart of museum country where hearts and souls can fall in love with life again in a bigger, newer way as you climb across new vistas . . . where you will walk with us into history by living the legacy of those who came before.

I repeat, I am not making this up. I don't really need to deconstruct this smarm, point out that development infrastructure kills wildflowers or that elk, now an overabundant species because of predator annihilation, will eat your indigenous plantings, or that the coyote is not a cute little gal with upturned snout and red bandana but a verminous, snarly true daughter of the wild who will gobble Boopsie, your Yorkie, in a high desert heartbeat. No, the realtor's unfortunately deathless prose speaks for itself . . . and speaks . . . and speaks . . . and speaks.

Perhaps more restrained, but nonetheless telling, is an ad for Flagstaff's only gated community's new expansion. The corporation decided to gouge a second golf-course gated development into a rare intermittent wetland valley one mile from its existing golf-course fortress, built during the late 1980s. Here's its paean to the new destruction: "Thousands of years of nature—on mountain peaks rising above pine trees thick with clear skies and sunlight."

Huh?

A decade of golf so rich in view and challenges it is rated number one in Arizona. A decade of families [over 75 percent of the second and third homes lie unoccupied for six to eight months of the year, and only a tiny percentage are occupied by families consisting of more than Mom-and-Pop Got-Rocks Retirees] creating traditions that will be relived and retold for years to come. And now, the natural unfolding of the next generation. More of the same remarkable things that made the first generation what it is: Forest Meadows. Wonderfully and incomparably Forest Meadows.

Please, who writes this stuff? More crucially, who reads and is beguiled by it? Much as I am critical of the rich, I never equated wealth with ignorance and illiteracy. Until now. Now, wonderfully and incomparably tasteless. Wonderfully and incomparably dumb.

It would be nothing but tragically funny if it weren't for the brutal fact that more than a thousand moderately high-priced houses are not selling in our town and the half-million-dollar homesites—that's home*sites*, not homes—are. And the pornographers who create—rather, *destroy*—these developments have an eye for the most beautiful, wet, and wild locations. Wetland by wetland, arroyo by arroyo, habitat by habitat, desert bighorn by desert bighorn, we are losing the best of the best. All for huge profit, all so that rich, clueless buyers can own a bizarre mix of the "wild" and the blandly secure: "Your own Hohokam petroglyphs in a desert canyon paradise. And the really exciting part, all of this with private security force" (for a gated community outside Tucson).

I consider the definition of *pornography*—words and images used to sell the body—and I remember Terry Tempest-Williams's words: "This isn't real estate. . . . This is the body of the beloved."

I invite any of you intrigued by real-estate porn to let your *road-journey life map* take you back to the nest you have contributed to fouling. And I am available at an exorbitant fee (90 percent of which will go to grass-roots land trusts) for ethical-writing in-service workshops for public-relations firms.

Running Out

I drive south, then go east on the Carefree Highway. Cholla catches morning light, a floss of white-gold. Few flowers this year. It's been a dry winter. I think of water. Of how the aquifer might once have been. I wonder how this desert might have looked five hundred years ago. Later, in Globe, a painter will tell me that when Coronado came through these lands, grass grew up to the bellies of his horses. Now, For Sale signs sprout everywhere. West of the turnoff to Scottsdale Road, a fence hides what lies behind it and a sign says Sierra Encanto (should be Sierra *Destructo*) Construction Entrance.

Years ago, I passed an agave on a hike up to Bear House. Coming back in the near twilight, we all swore that the agave had grown a foot. It seemed a miracle. This clear morning, looking south toward the city, I see a brown haze moving north. I pull over, look back down the highway at the parade of For Sale signs. I look through the crack in the construction entrance. There is nothing miraculous in *this* growth. Nothing.

I am going into the city to sit in a circle of women and write about aging and, the next day, passion. I wonder what passions will emerge.

I think of my course description:

> Passion lives in these holy places: anger, sorrow, terror, despair; if you don't run, passion will emerge. From these deserts of the soul—just as we name "badlands" the country where light burns deep in fleshy rock, glitters maniac in the rapids of high desert rivers, bounces fierce and dangerous off the back window of a pickup screaming west on a dead-hot Mojave highway. Soul desert—where passion lives, where stories lie like garnets, waiting for the light, waiting for release and gratitude.
>
> We will write from our passion for the earth, for justice, for cutting through. We'll talk about where to send our work, how to move our passion out into the greater world, to use our writing as a wake-up call, an organizing tool.

The city coalesces, congeals itself around big-box after big-box. I wonder if the circles I teach are making ready to move beyond self-exploration. I hope there will be women writing in anger, for justice, for publication, if not in books or magazines then in broadsides tacked to telephone poles, left in coffee shops, handed to people on the streets.

I remember the tattered flyer I saw pasted to a building in Chicago's Loop: "We must honor the rich . . . for their persistent efforts to go through the eye of the needle." I remember my astonishment and delight. Will my students astonish me? Will I astonish them?

I consider the brown haze above acres of enchantment for sale, acres of enchantment ripped to shit. I turn onto Scottsdale Road. To my right, to my left, perfect green lawns stretch for blocks. We have carved the pale, dry sand into resorts, golf courses, charming shopping malls. No one walks. Car after car holding one person stream by me.

We eat the desert. We are stuffed and we are starving. The desert is running out. Time is running out. None of this is news.

I am ready to be astonished. I am ready to hear my students tell me that they are writing for their lives—and more. I am ready to hear them tell me they are writing for earth, for jackrabbit, horned toad, and snake, for ocean, for the eleven-year-old hooker on the corner of some big-city street. I am so ready I ache.

I think of passion. I am afraid it is running out.

Compromise: *Ghost Dance of the New West?*

What the white people don't know is that the Ghost Dance really worked.

—ADRIAN C. LOUIS, "Earth Bone Connected to the Spirit Bone"

One hundred and eight years ago, Plains Indian people faced slow, painful extinction on government reservations. Wovoka, a Paiute seer, emerged and taught that by working hard, living in peace, and doing the Ghost Dance, the Indians could make buffalo and other game return in great numbers, dead relatives and friends live—and white men vanish from the earth.

The white men became uneasy over the growing numbers of Ghost Dancers and retaliated viciously. The Indians danced and sang as they had been taught. They went into battle believing that those wearing Ghost Dance shirts would not be harmed. The shirts were painted with sacred creatures, with eagles and dragonflies and stars. Now and then, you come upon one of these shirts in a museum display or hanging on the wall of a wealthy collector. The paint seems to glow. As do the bloodstains.

A few weeks ago, a county worker walked me over possible routes for the extension of Flagstaff's urban trail system. We skirted what had once been a place where locals hiked and walked their dogs, a place being dozed and dynamited into a gated golf-course development. We smelled the stink of asphalt and listened to the constant whine of heavy equipment. I told her that the roads were being laid, the earth rammed into the unearthly curves of a golf course, the intermittent stream fully buried. I said I walked hospice there every few days and filled my heart, not with the peace I had once experienced, but with sorrow.

"Yes," she said, "but you have to remember that the developers were the first ones to make a concession to the rest of us."

I was quiet.

"You can't discount," she said, "that they promised to give ten thousand dollars for work on the urban trail."

"Ten thousand dollars. The lots are going for half a mil; the golf-course membership, who knows what that'll cost?"

"I know," she said. "I know. But the old days of protest and confrontation are over. These are the days of partnership and compromise." She paused. "And they hold all the cards. No matter what Planning and Zoning might want to see happen, no matter what the Open Space and Greenways Plan determined, we can always be sued for a takings."

A few days later, I told a friend about negotiations beginning to save another precious place, negotiations that would require much compromise. My friend, a local historian, a man who can chip flints and surf the Web with equal grace, e-mailed: "The negotiations of which you speak, of what nature are they or is it related to the conquest of the new west? I know that the waves of empire have crashed against the coast of California and that now we have new settlers and conquerors of the land. Are we now the Indians? I ask. Where is our ghost dance?"

I thought of the so-called treaties of a hundred, a hundred fifty years ago, and John E. Mann's letter to *Sierra* magazine:

> When it comes to extremism, nothing comes close to our free enterprise system. . . . It is a mindless machine, its own internal logic pushing inexorably to overcome competition, to get the most for the least. It is perfectly made for converting a wilderness into a place of safety for human beings. . . . Against the power of this machine, what seems like *compromise* is in reality a giving of ground to a force for which giving ground means only slowing down a little.

How can there be partnership when one side holds all the cards? How can there be compromise when every compromise yields only loss of more land, more trees, more habitat, and more silence? In response to one of my recent columns, an activist in Colorado writes that her father, a man who made his huge wealth from development, is retiring at fifty-two.

"He is afraid," she says, "he won't be able to survive on $100,000 a year . . . and he'll be bored with nothing to do."

How can we cooperate with people driven by terror of emptiness, of precisely that which we find in the Big Empty, and which precedes understanding and connection with the earth?

Are we, who want to save what is left of the West, Ghost Dancing? Do we wear shirts painted not with sacred symbols but with the words *compromise, partnership, communication*? Would we rather gather in air-conditioned hotels and woodsy retreats, talking, talking, talking, than stand in front of construction sites with signs that say Development Kills the West; or slog through the numbing work of creating citizen initiatives, changing legislation, confronting, day after day, those who cannot listen, cannot stop in their frantic gathering of more?

Can we see it is not us, the New West Ghost Dancers, who are dying? Can we face that the victim lying beneath us, around us, annihilated by the hands of those whose weapons are not guns but, as poet Bill Ehrhart has written, "infinite amounts of money, time and greed," is the very earth that gives us life?

Don't Tell

I returned recently from a road trip in a corner of a state I won't name, a place of oceanic sage, 360-degree mountain horizons, cow-seared range, towns blessedly without charm, free hot springs lovingly tended by locals, heron and egrets and yellow-headed blackbirds, hard winds that flay the heart and blow away even the first notion of ranchettes, gated communities, executive golf courses. I came back into Flagstaff straight into the 1-17/40 nuclear zone, then down Highway 89A, where a new pipeline is burrowing under what used to be pine and limestone outcroppings.

My first phone call, a friend told me the news. "Zach lost by thirty-six votes." She told me the voting stats—only 17 percent of the registered voters showed up at the polls. The city council gone from Green to Greed. Seventeen percent! I thought of days and dollars of work on Dry Lake, Zuni Heights, the Peaks, *Open Space and Greenways, The 20/20 Vision Statement*—and how a few dozen people not spending fifteen minutes apiece to vote has rocked what balance we had fought for.

Who are we? What have we forgotten? What have we become?

A few days ago, I sat in one of those little unnamed hot springs across from a man home for a family reunion. He was in his late sixties, so he did all the talking. His father had built and partly owned one of the smaller dams on the Colorado River and passed it on to his son. The man talking at me was an expert in western water rights. I had managed to slip in that I was a writer and an environmentalist. He blessed me and told me it was hopeless.

"You know what runs the show," he said.

"You tell me," I said, as though there were any doubt he wouldn't.

"Greed. Pure greed." His massive double-cab truck gleamed in the parking dirt.

"I was afraid of that," I said wryly, or attempted to. He cut me off.

"That's just how it is," he said. "You won't believe this, but I'm one of the people trying to stop some of the growth in my neck of the woods. I am part of the decision-making on who gets water for development." He laughed.

"Hey," his red face grew serious, "you gotta promise me you won't tell anybody about this spring. We don't want it ruined." His son, floating near us in the silken water, nodded.

"No problem," I said. "We've already ruined enough."

He smiled. Then he and his son both told me they had been happy all their lives and that material comfort was part of it; don't knock it. Hey, the son would get the dam when the old man died. Success couldn't hurt. I ought to try it.

I thought of how the Colorado no longer runs to the sea.

They both wished me luck. I climbed out of the pool. The hard wind ripped across my wet skin. Clean. Honest. Not without pain.

Portal Canyon

I am in the heart of the earth, a delicate canyon holding dried grapevines, petroglyphs, cigarette butts, bottle caps, and a trickle of water no wider than my hand. I won't tell you how to find this place. Know that it is within range of the vampire lairs of Vegas and Laughlin. Know that from the throat of the canyon, you can watch a three-quarter moon fall slowly to a lilac horizon. Know that I am here to mend a web and to say, "Thank you," the two tasks inseparable.

I set my bundle on a dark boulder. My night-sky bandana holds sage from Butler Wash, a glass egg, a chunk of garnet, a chert scraper, a bottle of snowmelt from Red Mountain, and four hornblende pebbles from the same place. Some of this will go home with me; some will not. I prepare to light the sage, turn to the west, to the home of She-Who-Eats-That-Which-Is-No-Longer-Necessary, and see a woman walking toward me. She is pale, dark haired, and slender. She wears stone-washed jeans, expensive leather boots, and a faded jacket, and carries a bundle of silver sage.

Bear with me. This is not about Two White Chicks Sitting Around Talkin' Crystals.

We look at each other. "Oh," she says, "we both have sage." I am pissed. I want to be alone. I have work to do, water to leave, water to gather, pebbles to bury in the sand. She waits. Her eyes are hugely sad. "Is there water up there where you are?"

The words leave my mouth. "Do you want to come in here?"

"But you got here first."

"It's okay." I wonder why I say these things. "Come in."

She climbs into the boulder chamber. "I don't know if I should be here, but it must be okay if you invited me." She looks at me with those friggin' Seeker eyes. She tells me her name, that she lives in California, that she is so happy to finally be here, though she is always afraid when she knows it is time to come here and she had to make herself get up from the slots to come here and she didn't want to, but now . . .

I nod. "I know exactly what you mean."

We light our sage, give each other smoke, give smoke to the rock and silence and light. I tell her I am grateful that there is water here because a month ago there wasn't.

"What could have happened to it?" she says vaguely. I know she is used to asking questions for which she doesn't hear answers.

"You know," I say. She shakes her head.

"All the development, the casinos, the malls, the houses—this is desert, the water has to come from somewhere."

Her eyes don't meet mine. She is gone. I stop talking.

"Did you come here so you could stop gambling?" she asks.

"No," I say, and I wonder if she knows something I don't.

She tells me she has worked with an Indian shaman, has rediscovered her Mexican roots, is wondering about her Indian roots.

"How," I ask, "do you take care of the earth?"

"You mean these holy places? I give tobacco, my prayers, my thoughts—"

"What else?"

She looks puzzled. "What do you mean?"

"Where you live," I say, "are there holy places there?"

"I keep looking," she says sadly, "but I can't find them anywhere."

"What's around your house?" My voice is harsh.

"What do you mean?"

"Is there a lawn, a garden, flowers? How do you take care of them?"

"Not enough," she says sadly.

"Well, then, what's under your house?"

"I don't know."

This woman is at least forty-five years old, intelligent, curious, knows to come here, knows that holiness exists and a place can be holy, and she has no idea on what she lives.

"Under your house," I say fiercely, "what is under your house?" She looks at me as though I have the big mystical answer that is going to change her life. There is a long silence. I want to cry.

"Dirt," she says. "There's dirt under my house."

"What else?"

"Nothing," she says, "It's just a suburb, a subdivision."

"What about rock?" I wave at the glowing rocks around us. "What do you think it was before it was a subdivision?"

"Yes," she says tentatively, "rock and maybe water and maybe animals—"

"All of that," I say, feeling like a grouchy cross between John Muir and Shirley MacLaine, "is no more or less holy than this place we're standing in."

"Yes," she says, "I see. I see what you're saying." She tells me she knows she can do something for the lawn. She pauses. I know she wants me to ask her what that is, as a child might come to you with precious new knowledge and want you to honor that knowledge with your questions.

"What?" I say gently.

"I can let it grow."

We both laugh, a sound as soft as the light going gold around us. And as suddenly as we have begun, we are finished. I hand her my sage. She hands me hers. She turns and is gone. I finish what I have come to do.

A day later, I am driving toward the mountains of my home, the sun's last copper burning in the rearview mirror. I am thinking about the gifts she gave me: silver sage, questions, and the knowledge that at least one woman exists who loves the earth and did not know she lives on it.

On the Street—2000

I'm not in Seattle. I'm not young. Flagstaff is a growing Arizona mountain town. In a month, I will be sixty. Most every day at two o'clock, I stand on the sidewalk in front of a huge corporate bookstore at the intersection of Old Route 66 and the main drag. This corner was once the site of Andy Womack's Flamingo Motel, a shocking-pink joint within easy walking distance of the local bars, where a four-hundred-pound desk clerk with a parakeet on his shoulder took your fifteen bucks and handed you a room key with a pink plastic tag.

I am here with a very few of my friends. We carry signs and hand out flyers urging people to boycott the big-box bookstore and buy local. My sign, in a tribute to the past, is lettered in bright pink on a black background. It infuriates a lot of the folks passing by.

Once, those drivers had a clear view of the San Francisco Peaks. These volcanic beauties rise graceful as Fuji against our fierce blue skies. Now, this building that a friend calls a "colonial fortress" and others have nicknamed "The Ashtray" blocks the view. Tourists, not knowing what they are missing, signal and pull into the big-box parking lot. Some of them smile. Some of them open their windows and ask for a flyer. Some hold their heads very still, looking straight ahead, as if the sight of us will turn them to stone.

Others, not tourists, fill the parking lot hour after hour, day after day, a flood of cars I've never seen in the parking lots of our local bookstores. Others, not tourists, tell us they agree with us, but it takes so long to order books and the big-box has such a huge selection, and besides, you really can't change anything.

We almost agree with them about changing anything, but we are here. Nicky's sign says Boycott; Mike's, Keep Profits in Flagstaff. Roxane, just back from wto actions in Seattle, carries a sabotaged poster for *You've Got Mail.* Robyn's sign is bipolar—Boycott on one side, Support Local Business on the other. We grin and wave. We've all been trained in nonviolence, in the Gandhian business of turning the other cheek. So when the insults come, we keep our faces cheerful, hold our signs tighter, and mutter under our breath what we'd like to shout.

The insults come not from guys in construction trucks or cowboys or loggers. They don't come from Flagstaff old-timers or even from graying baby-boomers in their Range Rovers and Lexi. Ninety-nine percent of the time, the foul words, the brutal gestures come from young men, guys in their late teens and early twenties. And 99.99 percent of the time, the fingers jabbing the air, the faces twisted around crude threats, are white.

In an hour, I am told fifty times to "Go home. Get a job. Get a life. Get f—d." It is suggested that Nicky, Roxane, Robyn, and I sell ourselves for money, and that Mike is a lazy jerk. More than once, a kid points his finger out the passenger window as though it is a gun, pulls back the imaginary safety, and shoots.

"Get a job, get a life!" Nicky, Roxane, and Robyn are on their lunch hours. Mike's a wilderness ranger. My job, as a writer, is 24/7. None of us has enough hours in our lives to do all the real work we'd like to do, which we do pro bono, not just for three days out of the year, but every day, every week, every month—and which I, at least, do increasingly grouchily and, thanks to tens of thousands in solidarity in Seattle this last month, with the knowledge that I will probably spend much of the rest of my life on this corner or someplace similar. Get a life? Get the picture!

Of course, some drivers wave, honk, give us the thumbs up. In moments so rare they seem a miracle, a driver pulls into the big-box parking lot and does not go into the store. Instead, he asks for a flyer, reads it on the spot, and tells us we've changed his mind. In those moments, we know we are where we need to be. Doing exactly what is necessary.

And yet, when a twisted young face snarls or a kid spits or three cute girls pull a U-turn to come back and tell us to "Get f—d," I am afraid. Not for my safety, but for our country and its future. You see, the pink-and-black sign I carry in front of

the huge corporate bookstore, on the busiest corner in an
Arizona college town, blocked from sight of the mountains
that have stood here so much longer than any of us, this sign
that draws such venom reads Support Local Bookstores.

Super Downtown

Things fall apart;
The center cannot hold . . .
And what rough beast, its hour come round at last,
Slouches towards Bethlehem to be born?
    —WILLIAM BUTLER YEATS, "The Second Coming"

Our center is distinctly not holding. We learn from inside sources that for a year Super Wal-Mart has been slouching, rougher than any beast, toward the outskirts of Flagstaff. For what seems the zillionth time in five years, we call the zillionth meeting to stop the zillionaires from destroying our town. An exaggeration—more like the hundredth meeting, the zillionaires mere billionaires, J. Robson Walton, heir of the Wal-Mart fortunes, worth *only* $20 billion. Still, those of us who have loved our little mountain town for a lifetime or for what feels like one since we hit population of fifty thousand and the megacorporations began to move in, know that what we are battling *is* destruction.

We send out press releases, as usual, put up posters, as usual, expect the same dozen diehards, as usual. Most unusual, we open the library meeting room to *three* dozen unfamiliar folks. Old. Young. Anglo. Hopi. Retirees. Clerks and pet-store owners. Working folks who are fed up with the results of their labor piling up exponentially in other people's bank accounts far from our home.

We talk. We listen. We hear that Super Wal-Mart, upon learning that one of its meat departments had unionized, promptly shut down all meat departments throughout the country and began to buy prepackaged products. Most of us already knew that many of the items sold on the Wal-Mart aisles come from offshore and *maquiladora* sweatshop labor, but it is news that approximately half of Wal-Mart employees are estimated to be eligible for food stamps because the median income of a Wal-Mart employee is about twelve thousand dollars a year, and that many Wal-Mart workers are kept on part-time hours with no benefits.

We talk about the growing extinction of that endangered species, Local Business. But it is not so much the grim facts and figures that catch my attention. It is the woman who announces that she can't wait for Super Wal-Mart to get here. "I live on the east side of town and really resent having to drive to the west side for Wal-Mart [a twenty-minute drive on a bad day]. And frankly, I never go downtown. Downtown is only for university people and tourists."

I miss much of what's said next as I remember my own afternoon downtown. I am blessed to be neither a university worker nor a tourist. I write six days a week, often seven, teach writing on Monday and Wednesday evenings. My days of rest, aren't. Like most of us who haven't gotten lucky, I use my free time to catch up on chores. I am grateful that my years as a divorced and working mom are over. Those times make an afternoon of errands in downtown Flagstaff seem like play.

I'd begun at our state credit union, where Petra asked me how my novel was going. I cashed a check and headed over to Macy's, a decades-old coffeehouse next to a Laundromat presided over by no-nonsense manager Mary. I got the wash going and settled in at an old wooden table with fresh-roast coffee and paid bills, finished both by the time my wash was ready for the dryer.

I loaded it, walked two blocks for Dara Thai's elegant five-dollar red curry, ate, and walked to the downtown post office. The clerk asked me how my novel was going. I stopped in at Winter Sun Trading Post for osha wild-crafted by a woman taught by Navajo, Hopi, and Havasupai healers.

For ten bucks, Porter's jeweler fixed the catch on my late mother's bracelet and attached a charm. I browsed through McGaugh's hundreds of magazines and stopped at Pesto Brothers for fresh mozzarella (which cost exactly the same as rubbery corpo-mozzarella). The owner asked me how my novel was going. Mary had folded my wash for nothing but neighborliness. She asked how my novel was going. I stashed my wash in my truck and spent a half hour at Aradia Bookstore, gossiping, ordering a book on casino workers, watching the malamute and rez puppy tangle their leashes. As the light cooled, I picked up mushrooms and garlic for lasagna at Mountain Harvest and headed home.

Four hours. A mile of downtown streets. Thirty bucks. Priceless—a dozen conversations with my neighbors—in the coffee shop, at the bookstore, in the restaurant, the post office, and on the street.

Later, sitting on my back porch eating lasagna, I felt nourished. Not just by silken mozzarella and fresh garlic, but by something deeper—a sense of being home, in the company of people who want to know how my work is going, and whose work and future, the 24/7 of a local business, are very much my own.

Super Downtown, I thought. *A center we will hold.*

Super Wal-Mart, the battle's just begun!

Big Ditch

For eons, Arizona had only one Grand Canyon, our high desert ocean of rock and light, our beloved Big Ditch. No more. A second abyss is opening, ugly as the original is beautiful. Mid-January, *Pulling Apart,* a study prepared by the Center for Budget and Policy Priorities and the Economic Policy Institute, announced that the gap between the wealthiest and the poorest Americans is growing rapidly—and that Arizona is second for that grim distinction.

The *Arizona Republic*'s headline read: "Rich, Poor Chasm Widens." Imagine canyon rims, one lavish with landscaping, another stripped of everything. Imagine a retired couple living in eight thousand square feet of "Rustic Park Style" native wood and stone on one rim; a family jammed into a motel room on the other. This is twenty-first-century Arizona—Scottsdale, Prescott, Tucson, and Flagstaff; forests leveled, deserts scraped raw, intact neighborhoods bulldozed, rents so high that working people have to hold two and three jobs to make ends meet—a state where some mothers ask an advice columnist what to do with the surplus food they stored for Y2K and others flock to shelters for their kids' meals. A state where aging people buy new faces and bodies, and roughly a million Arizonans, one-fifth of the population—three hundred thousand of them children—cannot afford health insurance.

Experts tell us that there are reasons for the gap: Wall Street's bull market; rich retirees flocking to our golf courses and gated developments; low-wage service jobs replacing manufacturing work; indigenous people, students, and immigrants from Mexico and Central America working for minimum wage—and less.

The study understates the incomes of the richest, not intentionally but because capital gains—the profits made from the sale of stocks, real estate, and other assets—are *not* included (in 1997, the top 5 percent of American families received 75 percent of all capital gains). And in order to preserve confidentiality of respondents to the census, values of earned income above a certain level are kept secret—that is, 1989 earnings from longest job were frozen at $99,999.

So the abyss widens—and opens everywhere. New Mexico weighs in third, the poorest earning an average of $8,720 and the wealthiest $111,295. And although Montana ($10,762–$99,904) and Wyoming ($13,238–$108,450) fare better, the incomes of the middle fifth dropped 15.7 percent in Wyoming and 9.9 percent in Montana, the top fifth's incomes continued to grow. In Colorado, the midfifth's earnings grew 9.2 percent, while the top fifth's zoomed 30.5 percent, equaled only by Idaho, where the midfifth grew 1.9 percent and the top fifth grew 25 percent.

Beyond these figures are considerations perhaps more essential, because what lies between the dwellings of the richest and poorest is not the bright mineral air of our Big Ditch. It is the emptiness left after insatiable hungers have fed.

How much is enough? How many Range Rovers and Lexi? How many homes? Clearly not one. Sometimes two, not rarely three or four. Two-million-dollar mansions on half-million-dollar acres. Huge silent houses whose owners occupy them a month, a week, a weekend a year.

Flagstaff's temporary neighbors drive up from the heat of Phoenix and Tucson, play a few rounds of pricey golf, dine out, spend a couple of nights in "the cabin," and leave. They will tell you they have worked hard for their money—in a country in which over 65 percent of the wealth of the top 5 percent of the population is inherited. What they won't tell you is that many of them have made their millions from "developing" the deserts and forests in which their vacation mansions squat. "We have the right," they say. "It's private property. If you want to protect land, buy it!"

Their words echo across Arizona's economic chasm. "Buy it!" How? *Pulling Apart* tells us that the wealthiest Arizonans earned an average of $141,190 annually, and the state's poorest made $10,801. How do you buy food for your family, shelter, clothing, medical care, school supplies on $10,000 a year—much less land that goes for $60,000 to $500,000 a lot?

A few days after *Pulling Apart* was released, our local daily carried an editorial response in which we were told "rather than bashing the rich . . . be looking at ways to raise family incomes for newly arrived immigrants, Native Americans on reservations and other groups such as minimum-wage service workers." The following morning, I learned that Northern Arizona's only educational/job-training program geared specifically for "displaced homemakers" was gone. The same state politicos who gleefully announced budget surpluses last spring had slashed the program's funds. So much for trickle-down and bootstrap economics.

These days, it costs $20 per car to enter Grand Canyon National Park, to stand on the edge of timeless beauty, to be reminded of how fleeting human fortunes are. For those living on the wealthy side of Arizona's new chasm, the fee is a bargain. For their poorest neighbors across the shameful gap, it is 10 percent of their weekly wage.

flip

Fire Ants

We're at Lower National Campground on the Colorado River in the Grand Canyon. It's late afternoon. Somewhere around the dark curve of canyon wall, the sun is beaten gold, but here most of the beach is blue-gray with shadows. For hours, a steady wind has been sandblasting everything. Tonight's cooks have set up and are huddled under the prep table, drinking beer, not saying much, waiting for the wind to die.

We're all scared. Tomorrow we run Lava Rapid. Out of six boatmen, only two have passed this way before. Jed (the names have been changed to protect the terrified) hikes over to Upper National, hikes back, hikes over again. A swamper for a commercial trip is unloading there. We hear the moan of a conch shell. Jed comes back, hunkers down with the cooks.

"Crazy dude," he says. "Rowed it forty-six times, says it's eleven seconds, whoosh, and you're through. He blew the conch for us. Says it's lucky."

"Cool," somebody says. None of us is under thirty-five, but whoever says it leans on the second syllable. "Co-*ul.*"

I can't drink, and I've hiked myself punchy. I can't sit still, and I can't not. What I've been doing all the way down this river, ever since the flip—we don't say *flip*, we say *F-word*—at Rapid 24½, when I came up under the raft and learned that when you are *in* this river you are absolutely alone, is making little altars. Why? Who knows. I was once a Catholic girl weaving May flowers for Mary, and I pray to a She and everybody on this trip calls the river She.

All I know is that after I put a rock in each direction, trace a circle around them, and put my silver ring in the middle, I feel less scared. So I go to a spot shielded from wind and I look for the right rocks, as in micaceous, garnet, as in scraps of Vishnu schist tumbled down by Her. I find what I need, chert for South, obsidian for West, a rose-orange pebble shot through with quartz for North . . . East eludes me. I look East and see a round blue-gray boulder under a young cottonwood. Perfect.

I crouch, brace my legs, and lift. I am the *Enola Gay* over Nagasaki, I am the *Ranch Hands* flying above the A Shau Valley, spraying Agent Orange over teak and bamboo, tiger and deer, Montagnard village and American kids. Hundreds—no, thousands—of eggs cluster in neat rows in the sand. Hundreds of fire ants rush out to where the boulder once sealed the nest. I stand deadly with the roof of their home in my hands. My shadow looms.

I set the boulder down gently. I am wrong. Wrong. Fire ants race out from under the stone, shore up the eroding walls. I wonder what I've crushed; I know that some of my companions would cheer. I was bitten on the ankle, Everett on the shoulder. A fire ant bite is a tiny devil's kiss. It burns for days.

I'm ashamed, and I am grateful I'm alone. I think about religion, about worship for anything but Earth. I look down at my busywork, then up at the altar in which I stand, glowing canyon walls, ivory sand, dried grasses pure silver in the fading light. A fine, dry perfume rises from coyote willow and mesquite.

"I'm sorry," I say. "I won't forget." Later I go to the river. Last light burns cool in the blue-gray boulders. The river runs red, sandstone gone fluid. I crouch and piss, my moon blood falls scarlet as cardinal flower. Blood and earth, light and water, we are altar and prayer, here and in an instant gone. Essential. Complete.

Flip

My lover takes off just after midnight. For good. He is suddenly awake. I imagine him surfacing from sleep's river and, good boatman that he is, taking three breaths, heading into the waves, feet up, searching for an eddy. I turn on the light. His face is gray, and what's in his eyes is so far gone I can barely remember its name. I've seen him this way once before, on a brilliant morning in Marble Canyon, the Colorado River green as malachite. He sat motionless in the stern of the rescue raft. I would have gone to him but the boatman yelled, "Rapid 25 coming up!" As he began to pull for shore, I searched the flat gray stone of my lover's eyes and, in that instant, knew something about death-in-life.

As the door closes behind this man I may have loved as much as I love the canyons and red rock, the dusk and ravens and white water where we courted, I know more. Outside my cabin window, the April half-moon is brilliant on last fall's grasses. I see everything with the same shocked clarity that once focused rock, river, and half-drowned man. Now I see that the last two years have been the slow approach to another rapid, and in the last two minutes, we have washed through.

I remember the first time we said, "I love you." I was still fifty and he was not much younger. We had hiked out to a ledge on one of the sacred mountains that seem to hover over our town. We had been together five months, and in that time, we had courted not just one another, but also desert rivers, October's vermeil aspen, the high-desert mornings and sunsets of the Colorado Plateau. He'd taught me to row, to read the rivers. I don't know yet what he learned from me, not how to cook, that is certain. As we settled down between the ponderosa and cliff rose, the town below emerged out of the morning mist.

"It's temporary," I said. He laughed.

"I can see it," I said. "How it once was. How it will be again. When the town is gone. Just green and gray and red, just clouds and sunlight moving through."

"I think," he said, "no, I *know* that I have always been and I will always be. Maybe as air, maybe in one of these pine trees, you know?"

I turned and looked at him. This was not the man I knew, a man whose favorite topics of conversation were roof racks, the good/bad old days up near Da Nang, beer, and the infinite uses of duct tape.

"You know," I said, "in the best way—I know this will scare you but, in the best way—I love you."

"Me, too," he said. "In the best way. I would have said it earlier, but I was afraid you'd go."

He took my hand, pulled me up, and we walked back. The sun burned off the mist. In the dark-green shadows, you could still see your breath.

"Listen," he said, "I don't want this to bind us to anything, but that Colorado River trip next August, I'd like you to go with me. I want to do it with you. With *you*."

"Of course," I said. We held each other for a long, long time in that thin, cold, sun-washed mountain air.

August monsoons, the scent of pine steaming up from the forest floor, we woke and drove north to Lees Ferry, rigged his raft, and moved onto the mineral-green water, my lover rowing, joy blazing on his big face. I smiled back and saw that his eyes were not on mine. He looked past me, downriver, ahead. I bent and trailed my hand in the water. It was icy. I cupped some in my palm and touched my face.

That night, we slept apart on our camp cots. We had agreed—no tent. Just a sky neither of us had ever seen from just this particular beach, between these ragged stone walls, under stars and crescent moon shimmering in a ribbon of indigo.

I woke early and afraid. My lover said something nasty. I snapped back. "Sounds like a personal problem," he said. "Lighten up." I turned away.

We put in, moved steadily downriver, rapid after rapid. He was calm, as focused as he once might have been moving into Laos out of Vietnam. I was anything but calm. There was nowhere, in the midst of sixteen people, in all that redwall lime-stone, that compelling water and sun-bright balance, to loose the anger knotting my heart.

We scouted Rapid 24½, climbing past glittering purple rocks, past a boulder that seemed the shape and color of my rage. I touched it, the sun hot on its surface, in my fingers, cauterizing pain clearing my vision. I looked down on the river, and I imagined something knotted in the guts of the current. I glanced at the trip leader. He grinned.

"Let's go," he said.

We went. Into the tongue, in an entry so smooth that I lifted my camera and shot a picture. I have it still, taped to my fridge, a quote from Thomas Paine printed across the sky.

"Hang on!" my lover shouted. The world tilted, spun, and I was in the fierce water. Under the raft.

This is not a movie, I thought, and time forgave me. *Slow, slow,* I thought. *Remember Roxane. She came up under the boat, grabbed the cargo net, pulled herself free.* I reached up and hauled myself out. "If you flip," the head boatman had said, "take three breaths."

There was nowhere to come up for air. *This is not a story,* I thought. *One, two, three,* I counted, and swung my legs forward. Light glittered just above my head. I surfaced, gasped. An icy wave slammed me down.

Into vast blue-green, into light that was not water, was noth-ing known. I wanted to just go into it. *I'm fifty-one,* I thought. *This love's too hard.* That instant, a fine, clear fury rose in me, and in a moment of profound spirituality, I thought, *I've paid for eighteen days on this gorgeous friggin' river. I'm not gonna die on Day 2!*

The river spat me out, and I knew She hadn't done it out of pity, mercy, or anything but hydraulics. I swam the fifty feet to the rescue raft, the boatmen wrestled me in. My camera, my dark glasses, my amulets still hung around my neck. It ap-peared I had lost nothing.

And then I remembered. "Where's—?" The boatman fin-ished the question. "In back. We just grabbed him. He went down three times." I looked. I saw that gray presence, and I saw that he looked not downriver, not ahead, but somewhere else, and I knew it was a place I could not go.

Two years later, this August morning, our April good-bye four months old and solid as stone, I sit in my backyard meadow. Gila shooting star blooms scarlet in the dry grasses. I drink good coffee and think about that first parting, how he went west and I went east and we were suddenly as distant as the rims of the canyon walls. I have come to believe that I fell in love not so much with the man as with that high desert web of dusk and silence and glowing rock. And he was not so much in love with me as with dawn and river and the ways a woman, any woman, is so much like a river, so much like the earth.

What I know, beyond doubt, is that stone and light and water long survive love and betrayal. As well as death-in-life, there is life-in-death, in the hard sweetness of letting go. And I remember what is written across that photo, across the sky above the hole in Rapid 24½ of the Colorado River:

We have it in our power to begin the world again.

On and On

They say he is dying. "It doesn't look good," he tells someone who tells me. I want to call, but that is not allowed.

I remember his first death. He told me the story: going down in a chopper, no way he would survive, those moments of perfect peace, then nothing, then the smell of gasoline, and he knew he had better get the fuck out of there. The second death was below a cave in the highlands near the Rock Pile near Da Nang. He was on the shit-burning detail, piled it in a cave, threw on gasoline and lit his Zippo. The vapors caught and blasted him down the hill. He found himself hanging upside down from concertina wire, his pant leg on fire. "If I tried to move my arm to put out the fire, the wire cut me deep. But you know how it is. Fire always wins. I got my arm free and smacked out the fire." The 'Yards cut him down two minutes before the land mine, just under the wire, blew the place to pieces.

He died the third time in my bed. He turned and looked at me as though I were a stranger. "I gotta go," he said. "I don't have romantic feelings for you anymore." Behind his shoulder, a painting of Mahakala, the Tibetan God-Who-Eats-Everything, grinned open-mouthed.

"Done. Finished," I said.

He said, "We can be friends."

"Done. Finished."

Now, the fourth death. Four is the number of completion, and he is not telling me about this one. The Real One. How he will be dinner, and Mahakala will lick His lips.

He would think I was crazy if I told him this. He often thought I was crazy. Today he would be right. I feel wacky and furious. I want to make lists, send packages to people, send cards, make phone calls, do anything but sit here, trapped in my own skin, moving this pen over this paper, writing about death, writing about love, writing about the death of love.

It is beautiful here, brilliant soft October light, death everywhere, golden in the tall grasses, raven-black in the leaves of squash, tomatoes, and sunflowers. No, in the leaves of to-matoes, sunflowers, and squash. I change the phrase. Go for rhythm. Kill one riff, give life to another. Bridget wrote me about painting and death, how the pigments' pure colors die in being mixed. Writing is the same.

A man I once loved is dying. A man who once loved me will die. I don't know how long he has. The rumors were vague. And for three years, we have not talked, this man and I who woke most mornings making love, laughing, talking, telling stories we had told no one else. We will not hike the Ruby Mountains. We will not camp south of Cadiz, right where the perfect light meets the perfect sky.

I want to go to him, tell him all of this. I want to thank him for Cottonwood Canyon and Grosvenor Arch, for a perfect light-drenched, black-velvet twilight and dawn at Tater Point on the North Rim of the Grand Canyon, for making love on a tiny beach at Lake Powell and how our bodies crushed green reeds that smelled exactly like young corn—and I was com-pletely happy. I want to thank him for Da Nang and a rice bar up in Laos when American soldiers were not *in* Laos and the story of Montagnard warriors crouched in a circle, farting and giggling, when neither he nor these small fierce men knew whether they would be alive in the morning or not. And how he lived through all of that and tried to learn, always tried to learn.

I want to tell him that running the Colorado changed my life and that the flip in Rapid 24½ was an omen, how we moved through that jade water, surfaced, came back to shore in ways very different from each other. I want him to know that I love my way.

I hope, in this dying, in this living till he dies, he does the same. There is a great deal more. How our perfect early pas-sion restored me to my pleasure, how the last betrayals on both our parts reopened thirty years of wounds—in my heart, body, and trust. And I would not change a touch, a breath, a lie, a moment of rage. *We* were. And then a great black shining wing brushed past us and we were scattered.

All of it—pleasure, lake, river, arch, and canyons—was no more than beauty mirrored in a huge sleepy eye. One blink and you could barely tell "we" had come together and wafted apart.

I want to tell him all of this. And yet what haunts me are the words of my dying father. I had sent him a letter, told him I loved him, thanked him for the gifts of my childhood, some he knew, some he might never have guessed. I waited for a reply. None came. Weeks later, my mother told me she had seen the letter near his hospital bed and asked him about it.

"Oh, you know Mary Liz," he said. "She just ran on and on and on."

Here is, perhaps, the only question that counts: how do we love? I think of the years ahead. Letting the answer come shining out in my stories, twisting deep as canyons, burning hard and brilliant as the Southwest sun, running easy and fierce as a desert river. White water and pool. Shadow and sage. Diamond light. Crazy. Headed downriver, as you are now. Running on and on.

Coming Home

On my fifty-sixth birthday, I am given a poem by my grown daughter, Barbara's art, a videotape of my youngest son playing guitar in an Osaka rock-'n'-roll band, mistletoe and holly from Judy because I want the sacred plants reclaimed, a rose-gold hike with Michael at Grapevine Canyon, slot heaven in Laughlin till 5 A.M., a turkey-bacon monster Subway sub, and then, sometime between ten and midnight, a dream in which an old acquaintance turns to me and says, "Did you hear about Bill? Did you hear about Bear?"

I woke the next morning in my beloved house, began to write, and stopped. I lit a candle and set it in the western window. West. Home to She-Who-Eats-All-Which-Is-No-Longer-Necessary. New Year's Day, I had made an altar on the sill. Basalt from the red dirt and cinders beneath a downed ponderosa in Buffalo Park; a pinecone from its still-green bough because I had heard in late December that Bill's doctors could do no more, and I wondered how it was to be that tree, alive and dead in the midst of so much beauty; a little rock from Hermit Trail, red-orange veined with quartz, Bill had brought me from a hike into the Grand Canyon. I doubt he knew that next to the red-dirt roads and the luminous heart of beyond the beyond, it was the most precious thing he ever gave me.

I wonder if he knew the most precious things I gave him were words, while we were together and long after he was gone. Poems. Stories. "Luzianne." "Huevos." "Flip." The dedication to *Sister Raven, Brother Hare*—"For Bill, who knows enough to know he doesn't know."

And words he would never read: Big, indestructible Bill dying. Metastasis. The Bear on his way out. Heading west. The Death he danced with up on Route 9, into Laos, west of Lang Vei, that dancer taking him firmly in hand, turning up the rock 'n' roll, leading, leading, telling him he fucking well better learn to follow.

"I never met a woman who couldn't follow," he once said to me. We were paddling his canoe down the Verde, somewhere between the Bridge and Beasley. I was hurt. We had danced the night before, him drunk on Miller Lite, me drunk on him. I'm sure I didn't say anything, just stashed it away with all the other moments that killed my love for him—and his for me.

I set the rock in the candlelight. The quartz holds the tiny flame in its heart. I press the rock against my cheek. I want it to feel warm. It is cold as winter light. I know it's time to make a call.

"Bill is dead," the woman says. "Last night, about six."

I thank her. We say good-bye.

I sit at the old rolltop desk, and I begin to write. About Raven, Badger, and Bear. About tracks moving in, moving out. I write about the desk in the heart of where I live and my grandfather's rolltop and how its scent—pencil shavings, ink, tobacco—was pure life for an eight-year-old girl afraid of dying.

"I am home," I write, "wishing you farewell."

Buckskin

This is one blue-gray icy morning. I go to the outhouse and what I see while I'm perched on the seat is that somebody, probably the new granola chick in Cabin 5, has put up a sensitive poster. Endangered Species of Arizona, it says. There is a big mandala of animals and fish and birds, and below, lists of all the creatures that are on their way out.

My butt is freezing. I distract myself by reading the lists. I learn that among the endangered fish is the razorback sucker. I say the name out loud.

"Razorback sucker—endangered—you bet he is."

I think about him, Bill, my ex, the original razorback sucker, till I'm shivering. I pull up my pants and walk back to the cabin. Juniper smoke rises from my chimney. It is the exact shape and color of a great blue heron's wing feather.

The Cabin 5 Granola scuttles into the bathhouse. I remind myself to shower around noon when the patchouli reek will have cleared away. I can't believe people still wear that stuff. I've hung on to a lot from those days—cynicism in the face of government facts; too much ethnic jewelry; unease whenever success looms; a preference for scruffy guys in T-shirts, jeans, and work boots; terminal devotion to The Who—but patchouli is out.

I open my door and sidestep old Stretch, the brain-damaged cat from the farm across the road. He cusses like an Irish drunk. I dump milk in a dish and watch him stick his ugly nose in the plate. He mutters clear through this second breakfast and leaves without so much as a thank-you.

For a second, I actually feel good. Another ungrateful hung-over male dining in my kitchen; I've come in from a high desert November morning to a warm cabin that smells of coffee and fresh bread; I see smoke as feathers—no way this could be bad. Even if I am five years past fifty and a smart, not pretty woman, and the guy I made the best love with in my life is dying across town, being nursed by his new wife, who was once my dear, dear friend, and none of the three of us have said anything to each other for two years, eight months, and thirteen days.

I can't fix it. Nobody can. None of it. Bill is dying, not like I once wrote, from a heart attack while he's putting chains on the Cat road grader, so that he falls forward and waffle-prints his forehead. He's not dying because some jealous husband shot him in the balls, which is the most reasonable scenario. He's not even dying, unless you get technical, from the Agent Orange through which he must have crept on some ambush in some country we did not have our troops in way back when. Nothing as clean as that.

He's got cancer. Everywhere. All two hundred fifty pounds of him—or what's left of him, all six feet two inches, big wide hands, big wide feet, big wide, uh, whatever—*that* probably still works. And while I'm standing in the middle of my lonesome kitchen, looking down at Stretch's muddy paw prints and thinking about Bill's whatever, I remember the last thing I said to him. I'd heard he had cancer of the tongue, and I called him. I mean, the fool might have walked out with the wife of the couple who were our best friends, and I *had* heard they'd been fooling around for the last six months while the four of us played happy-couple pals, but cancer was *cancer.*

"Bill," I said, "of all places, your tongue, that hardly seems fair."

He laughed, the first and only warm sound I'd heard from him since he had climbed out of my bed at 1:21 A.M. on April Fool's Day.

"Just an aberration," he said in his business-phone voice. "No big thing. Struck me as a wake-up call."

Struck is exactly the word I think of when I hear that cancer has someone. You're walking along, minding your own business, when, bap, something less merciful than lightning slams into your cells, rearranges electrons, and you will never be the same again.

"Hello, mortal," Cancer says. "You are just that."

I've heard the cheery holistic babble about body-mind-spirit healing. And I hear that my ex-dear-friend is feeding her new husband, my ex, tasty vegetarian dishes and a rainbow of vitamin pills. They don't drink anymore. They don't, I hear, do much of anything.

I wonder if they, who hated how I gather sage and raise my arms to the moon, the sun, to whatever video-poker machine has just paid off, I have discovered prayer. I hope so. They're going to need it, because here's the truth: Bill was not a nice guy. He was a liar. A cheat. By his own words, a selfish pig. I figure he might have pissed off She-Who-Watches-Over-Love. And if She's there and vengeful, a few words and gestures from him and the wife can't hurt. Hey, Bill, pour a beer on the sand, give a nickel to a homeless vet.

Here's the mystery. I think of his wife chopping broccoli, browsing the vitamin shelf, snuggled next to Bill on the couch that she brought from her dead marriage while they watch *Barfly* for the twenty-zillionth time. I think of her nursing him through his dying. Being his widow. And, check this out, I feel sad.

Bill dies at 6 P.M. on my birthday. Only silence has moved between us. The only way I find out he's gone is I have a dream in which a mutual acquaintance asks me if I've heard about Bill. I wake and call another mutual acquaintance, and she tells me, "He died last night." I wonder about joining all the mutual acquaintances at the memorial service and dealing a Queen of Spades to the grieving wife. I don't.

I burn candles. I try to cry. I look at an old picture of my beloved in which he is hugely hung over and wearing a French crocheted shopping bag on his head. It was the night he howled, "I love you," and when I told him that I loved him too, he said, "Well, let'sh, you know, let'sh—" and I said, "Uh, how about one day at a time?" My one marriage proposal, and I blew it. Oh, well, I don't believe in vitamins, and I'm no sister of mercy.

Weeks go by. I do not cry. I don't cry about anything. Bill is the seventh in a series of deaths—my mom, my dad; Karen, the Colorado River goddess, and Preacher Fish, her dearest love; Bob-A-Kitty, feline Genghis Khan; and my belief that I'd never get old. My best friend, Ev, hauls me out on most of

Arizona's backcountry low-ways. It all reminds me of Bill, who first showed me all this impossible burnt-orange and cobalt glory.

"It's okay if you cry, Mary," Ev says.

"Yep," I say. And don't.

We're in Buckskin Gulch, Ev and I. Utah slickrock walls a hundred feet high, ten feet apart. We're at the phase of a hike where molten peanut butter and cracker crumbs taste like a ten-course Thai meal. Ev brews coffee, three teaspoons of high-grade per cup. He's stashed half-and-half in his pack, and he's looking a lot like God.

"Jesus, Ev," I say. "Coffee and peanut butter and slickrock, plus we found flicker feathers and a maybe-dead rattler—I am totally happy."

Two cups later, I can't sit still. Ev is sprawled out, grinning like the doper he used to be. He opens one eye.

"Coffee strong enough?" he asks.

"I gotta hit the trail."

"Go ahead," he says. "I'll catch up."

I head down canyon. The persimmon walls narrow, darken. There's been runoff working here for centuries. The water-varnished rock rises indigo and nearly shining. Above, a sliver of pure sky hangs steady. I stop. I think of Bill. The sky blurs. Tatters of clouds move in. I think of flash floods. I study the huge logs wedged in the walls ten feet above me. I remember wrapping my arms around Bill and whispering, "You're a big old tree." More clouds, vaporous as passion, drift across the slender river of light.

"Damn, Bill," I whisper. "You would love this. Why did you have to die?" I press my hands against the wall to my left, the wall to my right. I feel my pulse against the rock. "I am so sorry."

A cold wind swirls past me. I smell earth's stony heart. I am blown full of grief, brought to my knees on red sand. I lean back against perfect vertical.

"God damn you, Bill," I say. "I really loved you." I remember dancing to the truck radio just off the highway that curves down into the mist-green Verde Valley. I remember us, skin on skin, under a pile of sleeping bags on the November San Juan, sleet hissing down on the little river a few feet from our tent. And I remember cheating on him before he cheated on me, and the day I discovered an open six-pack of condoms under his bed, and me well past childbearing. "I love you," he had shouted then. "I love *you*, Mary!"

So what? I think. *All of it, so what?* Light burns molten pink down canyon. I dig my heels into the sand. "I loved you, too," I yell.

Something skitters across the trail. Lizard, maybe. Mouse. It catches impossibly in a thread of dry grass. It trembles. I crouch over myself. "Oh, go, follow the fuckin' wind," I say. "Whatever you are."

When I raise my head, it's still there. I make myself look. It's a feather, cloud-gray, barred with brown. Owl.

I am thinking of Bill. I am thinking of Owl, whom the Indians out here call death's messenger. I am crying. Crying.

"Leave me alone," I say. "I don't believe in you." I lean over, pluck the feather from the grass. I know, clear as the smoky light shifting above me, what I will do.

"Take it, you razorback sucker," I say, and I stand and cry and toss the feather to the hard canyon wind.

wild rose

Wild Rose

"Listen," she says, "I'm seventy years old, my husband's gone, he left me peanuts, and my kids aren't getting a nickel of it."

I'm at the Gold Strike Casino, a half-mile north of Hoover Dam. Her face is as hard and blank as the dam. We're playing quarters. I'm on Wild-Cherry. She's on Double-Diamond.

"This goddamn machine," she says. "Last week she loved me. This week she hates my guts."

Two weeks later, I drive Old Route 66. Basalt ridges stretch like charred spines. Joshua trees twist against a calcium sky. This Mojave is pure bone. I come down toward Bullhead City. The sun begins to drop behind the Providence Mountains, over Devil's Playground and the Old Woman Mountains. Below me, what's left of the Colorado River gleams amber. I cruise through town, past strip malls burning coppery rose in the dying light. Housing developments metastasize into the eastern hills. There are roads where six months ago there were none, and streetlights where once only cholla and Mojave yucca shimmered at dusk.

I cross the river into a million-watt kaleidoscope—emerald, blue, and silver, bright pink and gold; hotel-casinos, Colorado Belle, Pioneer, Golden Nugget; a cowboy two stories high that waves day and night; and you open the door to your room with a computerized card. The sidewalks are thronged with old couples in matching pastel jogging suits. Old women lean on walkers. Old men lean on their wives.

I park my truck, grab my lucky bucket of nickels, and hustle toward the Golden Nugget. A hound-faced guy opens the smoked-glass door. I walk through and am in a jungle. Brilliant turquoise water spills over polymer boulders. Parrots shriek. I smell river, Shinumo beach on the Colorado, coyote willow, tamarisk. Triple-canopy vinyl trees arch over me. I hear water and birds and, above it all, my crazy heart pounding in my ears. And then, beyond it all, voices, shrieks, and the get-over-here-now! clunk of dollar-slot payoffs.

A woman emerges from the dazzling light. She wears a

lime-green tunic appliquéd with gold feathers, fuschia sweat pants, and a plastic mask strapped to her face, oxygen pouring up from a cylinder clipped to her walker. I wear battered hiking boots and rock-climbing tights, my still-dark hair tied back in a faded bandana. We each clutch a bucket of coins.

She nods. I smile. I guess she is seventy-five, maybe sixty, desiccated by what chokes her. We meet on the wooden footbridge over the spotlighted stream. She stops, leans on her walker, pulls the mask away.

"Listen, honey," she rasps. "Wild-Rose was good to me."

I'm playing Piggy-Bankin', where three blanks on the centerline mean your bet gets dumped in a bank, and a piggy on the line breaks the bank open. The squealing pig on the video screen above us dances to the sound of breaking crockery.

"Listen," the woman says, "I've been on this stinkin' machine for two hours and the most I've hit is twenty. What the hell, they keep bringing me these wine coolers, so at two bucks a pop, I'm probably ahead."

She reaches out her hand. She's wearing five rings, all gold, one a tiny cat with diamond eyes. "Hi. I'm Rose. Isn't this the wildest?"

"It's chewing me up and spitting me out," I say.

A long-legged young woman in a high-cut leotard and high heels sways toward us. "Careforadrink?" She passes us. I try to imagine walking in those shoes for five minutes, and can't.

"Can you imagine," Rose says, "walking in those high heels for eight hours?"

"Hey!" she yells. "Wine cooler, honey." She drops five bucks in the girl's tray.

"Jeez," the girl says, "I mean, thanks." She wanders away.

Rose shakes her head. "They think old women don't tip. She doesn't know I was a lot like her."

I move on to the quarter Game-King, grab the only empty seat, and turn to say hi.

"Listen," she doesn't say. The left side of her mouth is slack. Her bright blue eyes follow every move of her daughter's hands. One quarter. Two. Three. The daughter takes her mother's finger and presses it to *Spin.*

"Look," the daughter says. "A cherry. You're a winner!"

She shakes her mother's hand. "She loves this. She had a couple strokes after my dad died. We have to feed her, bathe her, take care of all her private stuff. But the doctor said she's all there inside. Our regular helper quit, we had a free comp night here, so we brought Ma along. I put her in front of one of these machines, and I could see her light up."

The mother gazes at us. She blinks.

"Okay, honey," the daughter says, "here we go."

One quarter. Two. Three.

The mother's bright blue eyes are fixed on the spinning bars and roses and sevens. Nothing comes up. Her face doesn't change.

I'm in the Hurricane Zone. Dollar machines only. You gotta keep yours loaded, sixty bucks at least. Every now and then, plastic clouds above our heads slowly begin to circle. Thunder rumbles, the sound deepens, lights strobe, and we all go crazy. Anything you win between thirty bucks and four hundred can be doubled, tripled, maybe even more. In the lull before the storm, I'm going slow on Wild-Rose, hitting the *Play Credit* button every minute or so. The Hurricane attendant eyes me. I smile and shrug. The woman next to me laughs.

"Listen," Janet says, "you'll love my husband. He's a rebel just like you. Up till he started having trouble with his blood pressure, he rode a Harley, what he and the Boys call a Full Dresser, bright red, tassels hanging off everything. Twenty thousands bucks, would you believe it?

"Hey, he stays out of my business, and I stay out of his. The minute we walk through the door here, he hands me a thousand bucks and never asks one question. Don't tell me about those women libbers. I've got real freedom—

"I've run through six hundred bucks here, but my luck's gotta change soon."

Janet's playing three machines: $126, $98, $232 in a third.

I hear a low rumble. She jumps off her stool, stands rigid between the three machines. My throat is dry. The Hurricane strikes. I play one, two, one, two, up twenty, down sixteen . . .

Suddenly the Zone is dead quiet. We all look up. I feel like I'm surfacing from underwater.

"Shit," Janet mutters. "'Scuse me. God, look at this!"

$24, $101, $15.

She slumps on the stool, shakes her head. "I don't believe this. I never lost this fast."

"Hey, honey." It's the husband I'll love. He does that old-guy elbow-flapping motion that is supposed to indicate that he is, by God, on top of things. "Let's eat," he says happily. He flashes a roll of bills. "Blackjack was good to me."

"Honey," she says. "Jeez. Look at this." She cashes out. He pats her shoulder. "There's more where that came from," he says. "Win a little, lose a little."

"Honey," she says, "this is—ohmygod, I'm sorry. I can't remember your name."

Husband pats her again and turns to me. "She remembers what she shouldn't, and forgets what she should. I'm Fred."

He shakes my hand, looks me up and down, head to toe, toes to head. Janet smiles brightly. Fred invites me to join them. I am, however, up eighty bucks on Wild-Rose, so I stay put. Fred pats Janet on the butt; they both wink and are gone.

I'm out of the Zone. It's 3 A.M. I'm bleary-eyed, down eighty-three bucks, wandering from machine to machine, old woman to old woman, story to story. I can't stop. I see a seat open on the nickel Hay-Wire. I go. The old woman next to me is groomed to the teeth, and she is losing steadily. She turns to me.

"Listen, I wonder if I should've gotten started on this. I come here every day. It's like you read about. My husband doesn't know. He's busy with his projects. Last week, I used the Visa to pay the other two cards, We're not that kind of people. I mean, we go to church and everything.

"I keep coming back. I keep thinking I'm going to hit big, pay off what I've lost. I don't know. It could happen. There!

There she goes! Two double bars and a Wild-Cherry bar, four times sixty, two hundred forty—that's sixty dollars. That's something."

She smiles at me. "One thing I've always wondered. Have you noticed this? Whenever we talk about the machines, we always say 'She.'"

"Listen," I begin to say.

Listen.

Desert Tortoise, Meet the Annihilator

Lawanne calls in for my payout. I just hit seven out of eight on Game-King keno. Five thousand nickels. Two hundred fifty dollars. Which will, if I don't feed it back into the machine, let me go home down only sixty bucks instead of three hundred plus change. It's 10 A.M. The cocktail waitress brings me coffee with fake creamer, and I doubt I could be happier.

My money is slow in coming. It's Saturday morning at a Nevada casino whose name could be anything from Monte Carlo to Gold Strike—they're all the same. The busloads out of California began to pour in around 8 A.M.—dazed Asians, Mexicans, and South Americans, peppy old guys, hip-hop homies with their pants falling off their butts, all outnumbered by old women wearing tags that bear names nobody's given a little girl in seventy years: Estelle, Mabel, Velma.

Velma rushes up to Lawanne, stands directly in front of her, and says, "Lawanne, you remember me?"

"Sweetheart," Lawanne says, "how could I forget you?"

They hug, and the old woman heads off for Double-Diamond.

"She's one of my girls," Lawanne says. "I take care of her, and she takes care of me. Those Regular Ladies are like that."

"Have you worked here long?"

"Eight months, and I love it. Me and my husband came here from L.A."

"You were here in the summer and you love it?"

"Girl, my mama raised us in Florida. This is a—"

We say it together. "Dry-y-y-y heat."

"Truth be told," she says, "we have had us disasters, and I still wouldn't leave if you paid me. Last week, my husband was driving back from dropping me off, he works graveyard over at the Silverton, and our car burnt right up, burnt to a crisp. My husband got out okay, and two days later we found a beautiful Chevy Malibu with ten thousand miles on it for just what we could pay, so I figure it was just a little test from the good Lord."

I nod at the machine. "Same here." We laugh.

"I take everything and give it to the Lord," Lawanne says. "He brought us here, he burnt that car up, saved my husband, and he's gonna take care of us as long as I give it up to Him. We got an offer in on a house. I got my fingers crossed, but I just say to the Lord, 'Your will, not mine.'" Her dark eyes shine with a trust on its way to being pure joy.

I think of the acres of red-tile roofs stretching in all directions as far as you can see, how the night before, when I drove across the pass out of southern Utah on the long road down to Vegas, a whirlwind of light swirled up from the desert floor. I think of little washes minding their own business, cactus, creosote, bug, lizard, and hawk in perfect balance; and of the remaining desert tortoises lumbering at their ancient pace across the network of bulldozer tracks on the edge of annihilation. And I want Lawanne to get her house.

I slide a five into the machine to my left, punch up Black-Rhino, and start playing *Max Bet*. "I love that game," Lawanne says, "even if they've got those wiggly jungle-bunny masks. Seems like some people never heard of integration."

She waves at our row of slots. There's a Chinese guy, a Paiute couple down from Wells, a woman who already told me she's a born-again Christian and her husband would kill her if he knew she came here, a black kid in a DARE T-shirt, an impeccably made-up woman in a business suit (whom I will later watch at the ATM as she pulls card after card out of her Day-Planner to find that all have reached their limit).

"At least *we're* integrated losers," I grin.

Lawanne shakes her head. "Not losers. This is all my little ladies got. Most of them, their husbands are dead or might as well be; their kids are all over the place. What are they going to do, sit home and watch TV and wait for their friends to die? Uh-uh."

Manuel, the elegant shift manager, strolls up grinning. "It's you," he says. "It's about time." He and Lawanne and the busty black-roots blonde who always pats me on the back move through the triple-check routine that guarantees that none of them cut into the gazillions the corporation that owns this casino will take home. Lawanne counts a hundred, two fifties, two twenties, and a ten into my palm. I tip them out. They tell me that doesn't happen often.

Lawanne and I exchange addresses, phone numbers. I tell her I'll send her one of my books. "I wish I could just hang out a while," she says, "I love talking that spiritual talk, but—" She nods toward Candy-Bars, where one of the Regular Ladies is calling "Change!"

"Till next time," I say, and feel that double buzz of scared and excited I always feel when I think about next time. Lawanne heads toward Candy-Bars, and I slide one of the twenties into the machine.

That's the story, desert tortoise, that's the truth. We're the annihilators. Velma, Lawanne, Jimbo—and me. There are millions of us and a handful of you. And the only difference between the others and me isn't, at this moment, clear.

Chasing Sevens

This is our kids' inheritance.

I saw the bumper sticker the first time on the back of an old beat-up Airstream in a Searchlight casino parking lot, and I thought of one of my dad's favorite sayings: "Enjoy your money and your kids while you're alive."

He didn't, and died with that regret. I'm fifty-nine, writing is not work from which you retire voluntarily, and if I died this second, my kids would inherit nine full bookcases, a paid-for 1990 four-cylinder Nissan pale-blue pickup with raven wings painted on the doors, hundreds of audio tapes, and as many geodes, fire agates, and slabs, chunks, and chips of obsidian as you can fit in a two-room cabin.

I have 36¢ in my pocket, an obligatory $50 in my credit-union savings account, $43.72 left in overdraft privilege, and more bills than I can think about. There is one primary reason, beside being a writer, for my financial condition. Not shopping. Not travel. Not good works. I am a slot hog.

Nickel slot machines. Super-Sevens. Black-Rhino. Kitty-Keno. I read a checklist today that tells you whether you're a compulsive gambler. Four yesses means you'd better lock yourself and your liquid assets in the closet. I hit six out of ten, which in keno would win a lousy four nickels and in real life means trouble.

I'm thinking hard about all of this, not because I believe I can quit but because I spent three nights and two days of the holidays (Privileged Player Special—$39.99, free breakfast buffets, free drinks, and two free pulls on the Privileged Player Club special slot machine where I won a pair of red plastic dice) in a Nevada *gaming* town. Gaming is to gambling as *career opportunity* is to getting fired.

I was surrounded by old people, from the slot-machine seat upon which my butt seemed, too often, to be welded, to the Privileged Players Club, to the near-empty benches out back of the casinos, where you can watch a colony of savvy feral cats who have gotten so fussy they turn up their noses at anything other than shrimp or steak.

Most of the old people in the casinos are women. They have ten, twenty, thirty, and more years on me. Most of them wear pastel jogging suits appliquéd with sparkly kittens, Christmas trees, dice, aces and jacks, and logos from Palm Springs, Scottsdale, San Diego, and Atlantic City. They love to talk. Especially if their hubby is somewhere else, especially if he is dead. They wear big diamonds on their nickel-stained fingers, good gold jewelry, and sensible shoes. They rarely drink the free watery booze that the cocktail waitresses, most of whom are my age, bring around. They know everything about the machines, how to make the parrot in the parrot race go fast, how to rub Aladdin's lamp, how to chase sevens. When they hit, they cash out. When they lose, they pull another twenty from their purses and holler, "Change!"

They tell me everything. "We just sold the place in Palm Springs," the old gal next to me says. "We've got a double-wide in Tucson and a double-wide in Columbus. When we're here, we stay in a little park-model mobile home down near Topoc. We had to sell the house in Palm Springs. It costs a fortune to keep one of those places up, plus you know you can't get decent yard work done for decent wages the way you used to." Her husband plays blackjack. She figures it costs them about thirty thousand every winter. He won't admit it, but she keeps count.

Old women, old men, black, Native American, Hispanic, white, white, white, and me. Our faces gray in the hectic light of our machines, our fingers placing into the pockets of a very few very rich people what we believe we've earned, be it a fortune, be it next month's rent. I looked at the old woman's sweet face. Her eyes were warm. When I began to turn away, she kept talking. She set her hand on my arm. "My kids are all over the country," she said.

"How much do you see them?"

She shook her head. "They've got such busy lives. Careers. My grandkids. We get together maybe once a year."

"Are you close to the grandkids?"

"Oh, no," she laughed. "Kids are so different these days. I used to try, but once they got to be near their teens, I just gave up."

It was my turn at the counter. I cashed my points in for twelve bucks, considered leaving, and didn't. The old woman patted my shoulder and wished me luck. I went to the nearest machine and sat down. While I lost my twelve bucks, I thought about the word *inheritance.* And the word *elder.* By the time the last cluster of losing flowers and bells and sevens dropped into place, I knew that the inheritance we are squandering in casinos is not just money.

Those of us hunkered in front of our machines, bent over the craps table, hunched over a losing hand, are giving away our time, our knowledge, and our stories. What we might once have passed on to our children, our children's children, remains locked in our hearts and minds. We gather in casinos, in gated communities, in exclusive golf clubs, and leave the younger generations to piece together what they can.

Bitch Bitch Bitch

I jump in Ev's ancient pickup. "We're outta here." I shake my genuine cowhide Jackpot bag under his nose. "Forty-two dollars and seventy-five cents in nickels. That's an investment. I *gotta* hit."

Ev pulls onto the dirt road that leads to the straight-shot you're-gonna-get-lucky white line that's been pulling people west since Old Route 66 got reamed, razed, and reduced to a few two-lane stretches sprouting cheatgrass.

"You don't want to win," he says. "You want to saunter in, hunker down, and play till you get those squiggly coyote eyeballs."

"Hang on," I say. I bet Ev thinks I'm going to remind him that part of our deal is that we never say, "I think your gambling is getting a little out of hand." He shuts up, which you're supposed to do when your best friend calls you on your faint air of superiority. Instead, I jerk my thumb toward the mailbox. "I want to grab my mail."

Ev surfs March mud into the barrow ditch. I tug the box open and pull out the mail.

"Anything?" Ev looks chipper, the way you're supposed to look when your friend is a somewhat-known writer who might actually find a check in her mail.

"Oh, yeah, the NEA has set aside a special fellowship for me—a hundred K and a snake-hipped houseboy."

"The usual," Ev says, and we're off. We're loners who found ourselves neighbors in a cluster of substandard cabins near an Arizona mountain town, from which in thirty minutes in any direction you used to be able to drive to places of such beauty that you had to stop immediately, climb out, and thank the Big Whatever. Persimmon sandstone; black-sand washes whose basalt walls were filled with old scratchings of bighorn sheep, zero-eyed gods, and busty goddesses; a volcanic caldera where kids smoked pot and leaned back on the ruined foundation of an old dairy to watch a bald eagle swoop into her nest—all gone or threatened.

Now, when we head toward the horizon, we drive past Italian takeout clones owned by Pacific Rim corpo-mafiosi, bad espresso in every Stop-'n'-Run, and big gates that read, "Highlands Golf Preserve."

"Why do we need to preserve golf?" Ev always says. "We need to thin the herd."

I tuck a sheaf of unopened bills into my backpack. "I'm so glad we're getting out of here. Ten years ago, I would have never believed I'd ever say that." I open the map. "The Mojave. Cadiz and Amboy. Roads we've never run, pink hotels crumbling into the sand and Joshua trees and 1973 trailers with broken windows and the Old Woman Mountains and—"

"Laughlin."

"All-you-can-eat buffets for $4.99 and free breakfast because you're traveling with a senior citizen and then—"

"We saunter in and hunker down."

"Ev, my friend, it doesn't get better than this."

Laughlin spanks us. We're up, up, up, don't bother to eat, me crouched in front of Winning-Touch, Ev going red-eyed in front of Double-Wild-Cherry. Ev staggers up to our room at 3 A.M., $12.45 down. I drop on the other bed around five.

"Fuck fuck fuck," I say. Ev doesn't ask.

Lou Jean, our River-O'-Gold Breakfast Buffet hostess, brings us coffee. She taps my Lucky Jackpot bag. "That true?"

I raise my cup. "Let me get some of this in my system."

Lou Jean shakes her head. "Never mind, honey." She sets Ev's orange juice in front of him. She's got a ring on every gnarled finger, gold filigree and zircons, silver and chunky turquoise. "At least you got a free meal."

"Not exactly," I say. "More like a hundred fifty bucks."

Lou Jean shakes her head. "I lose that much every week."

An hour later, by some miracle, we are not in front of our machines. We are in Needles, California, looking at the map. Ev traces not the arteries, but the delicate blue veins. "Highway 95 to Parker, Highway 62 to Twenty-Nine Palms, cut northwest on the dotted line to Cadiz." Cloud shadow moves over the map.

"Incoming," I say. We're back in the truck before the hail hits.

I open the window, cup my hand. "Ouch!" I yank my hand in, set hail on the dashboard between the two-pound chunk of obsidian and the pink plastic My Little Horsie that Ev found in the bottom of his Circle-K Big Gulp on our famous Big Rock Candy Mountain trip.

Needles goes silver, City Midas frozen in light. What I love about this friendship is that neither of us turns on the tape deck. We don't talk. Hail rattles on the truck roof. Mist rises from the dirt street, the busted sidewalk, Ray's Car Stereo/Auto Parts, and the old cottonwood arching over it all.

Silence falls as sudden as Mojave weather. I slide in the *Spring '97* tape, featuring five reruns of Robert Plant's "29 Palms." "Let's go."

We almost make it to Parker. The tribal casino sign isn't that big, but it's right where we stop to make sandwiches. I feed bread crusts to the humongous raven perched on the sign. It studies us calmly with one glittering eye. "Here, dude," I say, "or dudette. You, yourself, must be a sign." The raven flops down onto the sand and grabs a crust. Ev and I look at each other wisely.

"It's a sign."

We head down a narrow road. Lake Fake glows like a Web-site beyond the little casino. I poke through the ashtray, find three dollars in quarters, and pry nickels out of the candle wax on the dash. "We *are* cashy."

We pay the gatekeeper a dollar and park.

There are thirty identical slot machines. You can play nickels, quarters, dollars, all on the same machine, which would be fascinating if we had more than three dollars and twenty-five cents, and if the screen didn't most resemble the beginning of a migraine. We split our bankroll and go to it. Four minutes later, Ev is up seventy-five cents and I am yelling, "I just hit twenty bucks! Let's go." We take our pay slips to the sweetly cheerful cashier and go into the glare of the hallway.

Ev stops at the door. "Wait a minute, let's check this out." He heads down a second hallway to a cashier's counter surrounded by blue glass windows. In the delicate gloom, we could be undersea, or in the middle of Manhattan. The air is heavy with cigarette smoke, bathroom disinfectant, and desperation, and I desperately want a straight gin. I have not had a gin and lime for nine years, three months, one week, and four days, nor have I found myself waking next to the kind of sub-animal lured by straight gin. Ev goes ahead of me into the restaurant. He is suddenly a black Ev cutout against an aniline brilliance of tinted windows, lake view, and desert hills crammed with mobile homes on the far shore. He turns. For an instant, I don't know who he is. "Hey," he waves.

I am paralyzed. Ev grabs my elbow. "Let's get out of here." He steers me to the door and through.

I sit on the cinder-block border of a dozen carefully spaced petunias. "Jesus, I want a drink."

"We are leaving *now.*" Ev starts to walk away.

I stick my finger in the petunia dirt. It's wet. "Hey," I yell, "but they take such good care of this place!"

We are back on the road. I tuck the twenty under the obsidian.

"What happened?" Ev asks quietly.

"You know." I look straight ahead, a stunningly ineffective way to outrun demons.

"You want to talk?"

I make myself turn my head left, take in lilac shadows, turn right toward Ev's profile against a dove-gray tatter of mountains. "Sure. I'm fifty-seven years old and I gave away twenty-five years of my life and I want it back. No big deal."

"Remember," Ev says, "the Mojave taketh, the Mojave giveth back." He shakes his head. "What am I talking about? I'm forty-two, fifteen years gone. I'm gonna end up being one of those old guys on a bicycle with a milk crate duct-taped to the handlebars and a mangy old dog riding in it."

This worries me. "What's so bad about that? I thought that was what you wanted."

"You ever really look at them? They're lonely. All they've got is that dog and the road, no friends, no one to come home to."

"You mean you won't get laid."

His silence is as hard as the land around us. I shut up. We miss the turnoff to Cadiz three times, get it right on the fourth. Long winter light holds, a dry lake shimmers moonstone.

I sing along with Plant.

Ev gives me the same look my kids used to when I would begin to sing.

"Hey," I say, "guess what was in *Modern Maturity*?"

"Huh?"

"The magazine for seniors. I joined. I did it for the discounts. Come on, Ev, ask me."

"What was in, I'm not sure I want to know, *Modern Maturity*?"

"Robert Plant's picture. He just turned fifty. His hair's all permed out and he looks pretty good."

"That, in case you're trying to cheer us up, is the most depressing thing you could possibly have said."

"Ev, how bad is our life? How bad is this?" I wave at the opal-shadowed big empty around us. An old salt plant rises from the glittering sand, rusted-out trucks and trailers gone bronze in the dying sun, broken windows shards of diamond.

"What I love about this Mojave," I say, "is that sometimes you can't tell if a thing is abandoned or still operating."

"Kinda like our luck," Ev says.

He snorts. I realize I'm grinning.

"Look." Ev points west. A great white gash shines across the blue-black mountains. "How can a mine be so beautiful?"

We come to the dugout as the sun begins to drop behind a rolling mystery range.

"Stop!" I yell.

We climb out, and Ev goes into the broken doorway of the dugout. Later, he'll tell me it was cool inside. The air smelled, to his surprise, not of piss but only of damp earth. He imagined miners living there, taking refuge from the withering sun.

"I wanted to crouch on the dirt floor," he'll say, "rest my

arms on the low plank table, rest my head on my arms, and just go to sleep." He'll say he saw my legs moving just beyond the entrance and he realized he was glad, for once, that he wasn't alone.

I don't follow him in, not out of any particular respect for his privacy but because I have just stubbed my toe on a battered KLM flight bag.

"Ev," I whisper, "Ev, get out here. It's happened again."

He surfaces from the shadows. "I don't believe it."

I stare up at him. I am crouched over the flight bag, and I hold a fistful of magenta satin. It is a low-cut chemise trimmed with black lace.

"The bag is filled with this stuff," I say. I pull out ivory silk and emerald velvet, black crotchless panties, a white underwire bra laced with purple satin.

Ev starts to touch the chemise and pulls his hand back. "The white Levi's," he says.

We'd camped near a little casino in early winter. Just past dawn, walking, swilling camp coffee, chewing over our mutual disasters, we found a rusted truck chassis shot to lace and, scattered over it, a woman's Levi's and blouse, bra and panties, sneakers and socks—maybe once white, maybe bleached by the implacable Mojave sun. We looked for bones and found nothing.

Now I laugh, a high, choked sound. "What is going on?" I rummage in the bag and pull out one black stocking. Woven in white, the word *bitch* repeats again and again. You can imagine *bitch bitch bitch* spiraling up a long, slender leg, and you can guess how the watcher might feel.

I look past Ev and hold out the stocking. "Where is the other one? Ev, where could it be?" I stretch the stocking out, tie a knot, and pull it tight. Ev flinches.

He goes back into the bunker. I hold the clothes. I consider taking them home, washing them, giving them to someone small and voluptuous. *Bitch bitch bitch.* I know I must not. I think of Los Angeles a few hours away, Vegas, how a girl, a daughter, a sister, can disappear in the space of a bad blow job.

Ev comes up out of the dugout.

"There were a couple candles," he says. "And a bag half-full of corn chips. There was a big sheet of white cardboard, not much else except somebody had spray-painted stuff on the rafters."

"Stuff?"

"Nothing bizarre, just gang stuff."

"Nothing bizarre. Just gang stuff. Yeah."

I realize I have the chemise and stocking gathered close to my heart. We check out a rusted trash can near the doorway. Ev reaches in, pulls out a rubber amputated arm, the kind of creep fetish that kids go for on Halloween.

"Movies?" he asks. "White cardboard for the light meter. Gothic porn?"

"We aren't ever going to know."

I gather up the silk and velvet and satin, and I head west. The sun is nearly gone, the air silvery except for a streak of brilliant orange along the horizon. I walk through skeletal Joshua and backlit cholla and creosote bush scenting the small breeze. I watch the ground. A ravine curves toward the mountains. I walk its rim, studying shadows, boulders. Nothing moves. There is nothing bone-white, no stink of rotting meat.

"Just the desert," I call to Ev. He goes to the truck, sits on the back bumper. I see the flare of a match, the bright coal of a cigarette.

I drape the stocking around my neck and I go to work. I feel my arm move, my hand release. Up. Out. Satin shimmers in last light, silk catches on yucca, lace on creosote, the magenta chemise on a Joshua. When I am done, I begin to walk toward Ev. He is nothing but shadow and a tiny red star that flares and dims. I unwind the stocking from my neck.

For an instant, I think about taking it home. I run it through my fingers. *Bitch bitch bitch.*

"Whoever you are, whoever you were, whatever has happened, I won't forget this." I crouch and bury the stocking in the cool sand.

Two days later, I call the sheriff in Twenty-Nine Palms. She takes the report. A deputy will drive out and check the place. I tell her the wind may have scattered the clothes.

She tells me she will call if they find anything.

grace

Grace

Today was hard. Safe inside these rough-hewn walls, I'm besieged by fear, the mean ebb of a brain chemistry ruled by genetics and fading light. Outside, there is no safety, there is nothing but the machine chewing up the West. I go to writing. Not on my computer, but by hand. Medicine trails out from my pen, onto the blank page, back into my sore heart:

My writing has not stopped the chain saws, the dozers, the dynamite.

It does not stop my pain. I can no longer legally walk in the meadow, scramble across the limestone, be in the presence of perfect balance, of horned toad, tuft-eared squirrel, hawk, wild onion, iris, and ten thousand other lives—in wanting vengeance, I have thrown myself into the imbalance of people, of egos (including my own), of someone saying, "That won't work" or "It's too abrasive" or "It was my idea."

Why am I back in the world of activism?

I'm bored to death with what passes for love between people. We've found and healed and rewounded ourselves ad nauseam. I can't listen to another liberal whine, hear another weekend Buddhist tell me, "We are all one."

And if I walk out tomorrow to the utterly familiar woods east of my cabin, I will see something I have never seen before. It happens every time, like a love affair that, impossibly, renews itself again and again. That's why I do this. How could I not?

Next evening, wanting only to be alone, I sit with my students in the tiny living-bedroom of a woman who has given up much for freedom. She writes about fear, about never knowing if her small paycheck will stretch to cover the big cost of living in a charming mountain town, waking each morning knowing she has only that waking, falling asleep wondering if the next waking will be the same.

I remember my first spooked greenhorn leap into the West, and I envy her. We talk about fear and how it is the huge room in which our writing lives. And, we laugh, no one is shooting at us.

"I don't know why I'm telling you this," Jane says. She is a single mom and a sign-language interpreter. Sometimes when she speaks, her hands weave story beyond story. In this moment, her hands are still. "I just learned about quarks. They are subatomic particles. They have flavors: up, down, strange, charm, and bottom. Maybe we are hunting for quarks."

"No," I say, "not hunting. We are waiting. Preparing. And sometimes they arrive. Like grace."

"Quarks of grace." Jane laughs. Her hands move, and we see desert rain shimmer.

Guadalupe Project

if every rebellion begins with the idea
that conquerors on horseback
are not many-legged gods, that they too drown
if plunged in the river,
then this is the year.

  —MARTIN ESPADA, *"Imagine the Angels of Bread"*

If the freeing of meadows and forests begins as you telling me how much you love this place, and goes no further, then this is not the year. If the protection of the West begins with you complaining about trees near you being destroyed to make room for townhouses, and you do not tell anyone but me, then this is not the year. If reverence for our home begins with you telling me not to leave because who else will write about the death of our home, and you do not pick up your pen, your good rage, and go public, then this is not the year.

If, as you tell me, you are ready to do something, a new year begins.

L. and I go to the meadow ravaged by Forest Highlands. We place a parchment prayer on the torn earth and anchor the four corners with *Virgen de Guadalupe* candles. The prayer asks the workers to open their eyes and see what they are doing.

We light the candles. There is no fire danger. Dry grass and flowers that might once have burned have been scraped away by bulldozer blades. The brush and small pines have been leveled. We step across the orange plastic mesh that fences a ninety-year-old ponderosa. We press our hands to the trunk and we say, "I'm sorry." As we leave, dusk settles and we see our candles flickering in the soft dark.

We pray this is the birthday of a new new year.

November, 1997, Dear Jason

Wherever you are, thanks for the slides of Dry Lake.

Every one was perfect: aspen shining gold and bone, lupine and globe mallow, shadowed wetlands, the peaks catching autumn light, right above where the Flagstaff Ranch Golf Club wants to put a clubhouse and golf course, wants to slash roads into steep, tree-filled slopes. You know. You were there. You've seen Dry Lake and caught its balance and beauty in your work.

Here's what's happened since you left. You already know about the phone call I got that Monday, the one in which a guy said he was the construction supervisor at Forest Highlands and that there had been serious vandalism. "And you're the prime suspect," he said. "Somebody put sugar in the gas tanks, broke windshields; me and my guys are gonna be out of work for a while." He said the sheriff would be around to talk to me. All this at 7 A.M.—before I'd had coffee.

When I called the sheriff's department, three different sources told me that no complaint of vandalism had been filed by Forest Highlands. And no sheriff came to talk to me. *Libel,* I thought. I hate legal stuff, so I called my editor.

"You know," he said, "I think we ought to take this to a higher ground." I can't argue with a guy who quotes Van Morrison, so this letter is all about higher ground, about the miracles that have come into my life during the last month of opposition to the development of Dry Lake, miracles bringing me solidly home to a town I'm proud to live in, a county I will defend with my breath, my voice, my pen.

"The pen is mightier than the sword" has become "The computer is mightier than the bulldozer," and the first miracle in this battle was the six-hundred-plus letters that poured from pens and computers into the County Planning and Zoning Commission. At the end of a hearing that looked like a 1997 Norman Rockwell painting, one of the commissioners said, "This is a real push-pull for me. *But the people of Coconino County have let us know they don't want this development.*" He voted to deny the Flagstaff Ranch Golf Club, a vote that put the decision over the edge.

A miracle within miracles: we wrote to our public officials—and they listened.

I think of that moment when the third disapproval was cast and of the shock I felt. I had not expected to be heard, much less to "win." And the "win" was not a simple one. Denying the FRGC's proposal meant that a 1982 zoning stayed in place, a zoning that would allow sixteen hundred housing units, a school, a fire department, and commercial development. "A zoning for broader community," one of the commissioners said. "Still, it hasn't been developed yet at that level, and my vote is the willingness to risk that it won't be."

All of us who spoke that night in opposition had no illusions: the woman who told of being fenced out of a place in which she had once hiked and gathered medicinal herbs, the carpenter who compared Flagstaff to a smorgasbord and developers to gluttons bellying up to the feast. We all knew that the battle had just begun.

Since that meeting, the miracles have continued, true *milagros* dissolving the despair of those of us who had begun to write this town and county off. What began as one woman reading an article about a "new luxury home development" and calling a friend multiplied person by person—mountain bikers, birders, store clerks, lawyers, rock climbers, gardeners, waitresses, old-timers and newcomers alike, all committed in word *and* deed to a broader definition of community. Without formal organization, mailing list, budget, or national backing, we divided up what needed to be done and did it. *The people of Coconino County.*

One of us would mention something we could use, and within hours the wish would be granted. "I'm a graphics artist. I can do all kinds of magic on my computer. Let me know what I can do."

"You need a data base. I'm great at organizing. Send me names and addresses and I'll set it up."

"You need letters. I'll call my friends. We'll have five hundred letters for you by Friday."

"Just tell me what you need. It's time for me to get involved again."

I have never had an easier time fighting. In fact, it has begun to feel less like fighting and more like loving—loving the fight, loving my companions, loving the fact that day to day I have no idea what will come next. All that love pouring into a little place, not a sexy star like the Grand Canyon or the Sacred Peaks but a somewhat battered wetlands, an old dairy farm whose buildings are scarred from years of disrespect, a meadow sustaining horned toads and elk, steep limestone slopes holding the bright shock of aspen and tiny plants whose names I do not know, tree swallows and dragonflies, ordinary bugs and birds, light, shadow, quiet—and connections.

Jason, I think of connections and of how we met. You wandered into the Inner Basin Camping Gear store selling jewelry, we told you about Dry Lake, you wanted to know more, took a copy of one of my columns, and reappeared the next day saying, "I'm in. I'm a photographer. I want to go out there and take pictures. If they turn out, they're yours."

I was the fifth person to speak at the County Commission hearings. A friend set up the slide projector. For three minutes, maybe less, your photos of Dry Lake shone delicate as a dream, clear as a wake-up call. I don't know if your work swung the vote. I like to think it did.

Good travels, my friend. Blessed be.

Mary, and Dry Lake.

Mile Markers

Northern Arizona is southeastern Utah is western Wyoming is western Colorado is the New Vegas, is native-log six-bedroom "cabins" where native forest once grew, kokopelli kandy booteeks, and shop-till-you-drop tourists hunting for the newest Tommy Hilfiger outlet.

It's easy to get here. Squeeze on the nearest deregulated airline and head for the setting sun, dropping blood-money red behind a thermal inversion. You'll find no surprises. You will leave wondering what you missed, and you will not want to return.

Or you can hit the road, the white line that carries you through landscapes of such raw beauty you'll be glad you're driving a beat-up pickup with a camper shell and sleeping under pure starlight. You will rejoice in the low budget that keeps you from the obvious, leaves you crouched over your camp stove, warming your hands at the coffeepot sending its fine scent into the high desert air. You'll pry the nickels off the candle wax on the tailgate and be joyful that a little casino lies just up the Interstate.

Mile Marker Mesquite, Nevada: I've driven twelve hours straight from Wyoming, down I-15. I am hungry and tired, and the lights of Mesquite sparkle like an elusive lover's promise.

The name of the casino doesn't matter. They're clones. I stuff myself at the buffet, dump my spare change in my Lucky Jackpot bag, and saunter into the reason for being there. My mind's on nickel Winning-Touch when I am stopped in my forward lunge by the last burnt-sugar notes of "Really Got a Hold On Me." A stocky guy is wailing the best r&b I've heard since Chicago, 1963. A long-legged woman hits the stage. "This is for the ladies," she says and slow-cooks into a seventies disco hit about freedom, her voice and the song going white-hot, the old guys and dolls actually turning away from their slot machines.

Later, we talk. Her name is Natalie. She and Daemine sing all over eastern Nevada, the Rainbow in Wendover, the Silverton outside Vegas, here, in a room covered walls to ceiling with black mirrors.

"We've been together thirteen years," she says. "Came here from Jersey." I tell her they're the best musicians I've heard in a long time and I wish I were a rich record producer. "Me too," she laughs. "But, see, this is just what we do. We have to."

Mile Marker Jackrabbit, Arizona: Headed east on I-40, my road-buddy Ev and I make the ritual stop at the Jackrabbit Trading Post. Billboards guide you in. "Here it is!" Little, black wooden rabbits crouch in a line across the top of the boards, utterly still, the way real jacks freeze at your footstep.

Once, a wind-torn black papier-mâché rabbit as tall as a short woman crouched outside the trading post. I am that short woman in a picture taken in 1982. I am grinning, believing I am, one mile off I-40, in the middle of wilderness. The ragged rab is gone. It's easy to imagine it swept away by a dust devil back to 1932. A bigger gray-plastic bunny with a saddle now hunkers in the dust.

Inside, shelves hold petrified wood, jackass salt-and-pepper shakers, and slices of geode dyed neon blue. You can still buy a cup of cherry cider. The Indian silver is tarnished and distinctly not mass-produced. Owner Antonio Jaquez polishes the bracelet you choose and tells you, "We want Jackrabbit to be true to what it always was. We believe in that."

Mile Marker Moriarity, New Mexico: Darkness melts up from the east. It is too late to walk in the little cemetery, to watch sunset fade from Eliza's headstone, the one carved with blossoms and spirals, the one from which two stone hands emerge holding a stone goblet. It is too late to read the names of the dead: Octaviana, Emilio, Luz; to see how rare storms have worn the tiny stone lambs to nubbins, how a rosary shimmers garnet against the dark rock.

We pull off on 1-40-Business and cruise the strip. The usual corpo-cuisine. Then a small sign: Bubba's Cajun Fish and Steak.

"No way," I say. "Not out here. Let's keep looking." The strip curves back to the interstate. We turn around and two minutes later walk into roux-perfumed air. A waitress carries a tray heavy with gumbo and a slab of bread pudding big enough to feed even Ev. We order seafood gumbo and a seafood platter. The food arrives.

Time and place shift. I spoon perfect spices into my mouth, dip fried oysters in sauce, wonder how I'll ever eat it all. We imagine the desert air gone wet and flowery, a southern river flowing past the door. There is key lime pie and bread pudding, and we eat past pain because everything is rich and delicate at once.

The co-owner tells us that the place is new. "We came here because we love this land. We do this because we love to cook."

Mile Marker Grants, New Mexico: Two days later, the heart of one of the last for-the-pure-love-of-writing conferences behind us, we wake before dawn, drive the dark web of Grants's streets looking for breakfast. Light and the perfume of baking pour from the Tres Marias Bakery windows. Two women move in the soft glow. We go in, buy two donuts, an apple fritter, one lemon tart, and four fresh rolls for under three bucks.

"You gotta raise your prices," Ev says. The dark-haired woman shakes her head.

"No. We love this. Bake all night, go home at 1 A.M., come back at six, probably sounds crazy to you, but this is ours. We've been here all our lives. This is what we do."

Rank Stranger

The big table is piled with food. We could be anywhere—the basement of the Methodist church in my mom's hometown, a 1966 anarchist picnic by a glittering creek in Upstate New York, a Save-the-Earth potluck in the early seventies. We're not—and we are. This last session of *Bridging*, my writing class for women and men, is meeting in an airy log cabin in the piñon-juniper forest east of town. We three women and three men have brought shrimp and guacamole and eggplant casserole, ice cream and cookies, and we have barely made a dent in the feast. Magic and Bandit, malamute and mutt, sit patiently near our feet.

We toss treats to the pups, winch ourselves up from the table, and wander out to the northern stoop. The Hale-Bopp comet rides fat, icy, and glorious in the northern sky. Orion and the Pleiades hang out across the way, who knows how many light-years away. Big neighborhood up there, just the way I like it.

"Can you see the individual stars in the Sisters?" somebody asks.

"I used to be able to," one of us aging wild things laughs. The dogs wind around our ankles. I go back into the house, a little uneasy, as always, from too much joy. I look for something to read. Earth, sky, and words are the only constants. Dana Jennings's dark-fired novel *Lonesome Standard Time* lies on the reading table. I open it to mention of a song not known to me, "Rank Stranger." I hear the voices of the students who are my friends, their laughter, and in that instant, more than anything, I want to hear this song.

Dogs and people come in, drop into chairs and couches. We write about the sky, guys made of stars, how the hell we got older. We read to each other, then Tony takes out his guitar and sings. Old songs, the music you might have heard at a Methodist church supper or an anarchist picnic or a tree-hugger potluck. I can't keep the tears from my eyes.

"Do you know," I ask, "'Rank Stranger'?"

He does—not all of it, but enough. His voice rises high and raw as loneliness. *Oh, yeah,* I think. *Some old-timer songwriter knew about loneliness that is not about too few friends, but loneliness for a disappeared place, a dead way of life.* Tony finishes. The room is quiet.

He moves his hands across the guitar strings. We all know the next song. And we are singing.

Wild Heart

—for the Flagstaff Activist Network

Good news: the Forest Service has begun the process of declaring our beloved mountains Doko'o-sliid/Nuvatukya'ovi/ San Francisco Peaks as Traditional Cultural Property. Good news: in Macedonia, Ohio, six McDonald's workers, ages fifteen to twenty, stand in the rain carrying signs that say Strike and Honk Your Horn because "a supervisor yelled at an elderly crew member and made her cry." Good news: the Dry Lake Website is up—www.savedrylake.org—and the T-shirts are printed. Good news: everyone who said to me over the past few years, "I feel so helpless. Nothing we do makes any difference," was wrong.

Good news: fire-rock mountains under monsoon clouds, drenched kid with a picket sign, wetland shimmering in the heart of a caldera, on a million luminous screens—wildness against the sky, wildness in the heart, wildness made no less wild by discipline and craft—all prevailing, all more insistent than whining and despair. I think about the wild hearts of my comrades in this earth-work, about the question each of us has asked: "Why can't I walk away?" I think about the wild hearts of many of my writing students. "Why can't I walk away?" they ask. "What are these words pouring from me, the words that won't emerge, won't obey, be nice, make sense?"

Wild heart's a harsh lover. Stubborn. Patient. Cruel as Kali's kiss, as compelling.

Wild Heart will lead you in. S/he draws the lucky into the interior dark, into those caverns lit only by fox fire. S/he breathes fire on your will, reason, logic, and good luck, till all have been consumed and you, the lucky, have fallen apart, fallen in, fallen out into knowledge for which there is no logic or will.

Wild Heart will leave you in your dark, holding the little child you once were, the adolescent you once were, swallowing the fool you have become, and gazing in horror at what you might have been.

"Good-bye," Wild Heart whispers. "Now, find your way out."

The mountains call you. Injustice calls you. Spotted owl and aspen and the blue May mirror of the wetlands call you.

"I feel so helpless," you whimper. Wild Heart laughs.

"It won't do any good," you whine. Wild Heart *caw-w-w-w-ws.*

"I am afraid." Wild Heart leaps off the topmost branch of the highest pine and shits on you.

You wait. To have enough money. To have enough love. To have enough courage. While you wait, the mountains are leveled, the wetlands are scorched by greed, the children kill each other, the old people sit, rocking to no music, and wait for Wild Heart to take them home.

Doko'o-sliid lies cobalt under a new moon. You study the snow tracing Her sides. You remember the pumice mine no less brilliant by moonlight than the snow. "Wake up," you read. "Wake up. The time of waiting is over. And you cannot walk away."

FOOTNOTE: In 2000, the federal government bought the White Vulcan Mine and closed it. In February 2001, it began the reclamation. Doko'o-sliid will bear one less wound.

Monsoon

These midsummer high desert days, I drive home under a hot noon sky, catch myself moving on city time, too fast, too mean. In a monsoon heartbeat, indigo clouds boil up over the western mountains. The storm dumps a torrent. I can't see the road and pull over into a fast-food parking lot. Three children pile out of the back of a pickup. Their long black hair shimmers. They dance in the puddles and drink the rain. I roll down the window, breathe deep, and listen.

In ten minutes, the rain is gone, the sky is a cool, cloudless blue, and I am on my way. I once sat out a twenty-minute monsoon hailstorm in the driveway to my home, opened my cabin door, and found the kitchen under four inches of water. Monsoons are generous in just this way. They annihilate. And they give.

The Hopi dance for the monsoon's blessing. For their crops. For the continuation of their people. And when their prayers are done well, the sky opens and we—human, pine, juniper, and bright corn—receive. I have stood, a grateful guest, at the edge of the village plaza and, as the dancers moved away to the edge of the mesa, down a trail we cannot see, felt the first fat drops of rain splashing my face, knowing that it has been this way for centuries.

Monsoons remind us newcomers just how small we are. They most often slam up from the south, but as a local meteorologist once told me, "Honey, they're like eight-hundred-pound gorillas. They go anywhere they want."

To live fully in monsoon country is to know risk—and to surrender. I write during a monsoon for as long as I dare. Lightning mocks surge protectors. One strike miles from this old rolltop desk can alchemize my writing into nothing as quickly as Hopi dancers fill the plaza and are gone, their footsteps vanishing in the new rain.

I give in, shut down the computer, and while thunder fades and rain murmurs on the cabin roof, I think about surrender. I remember how quickly I slip into city time and do not see the children dancing in the fast-food parking lot. Sunlight flickers on the wet grass. The thunder is gone. I turn on the computer and go back to work. As the Hopi dancers have long done, I am learning to dance to the monsoon—I go slow, stop, wait, and begin again.

Controlled Burn

My friend and I drive back from the Apache casino around midnight. Controlled burns glimmer in the forest. There is the pale shadow of an owl, two meteors, hours of good talk between two people who have lived next door to each other for years.

We talk about how hard it is to live in a world that seems increasingly alien. I would think it was my age, but my friend is thirteen years younger—as are most of my companions in this work. *There's no way out,* we say, coming around a curve and seeing a tall pine burning in the dark. We pull over.

The tree is pure incandescence; a tall and delicate Kali. Flames ring the base; sparks sail off on the wind. I think of the first meteor, fox-fire green, arcing slowly to the north. I look up. The sky is snowflake obsidian, Orion held in his great circling by our imaginations, his body no more than the story we tell about explosions of light.

Inhuman beauty is the perfect gift. Owls and pine, meteors and stars in which we see harbingers and goddesses, messengers and hunters.

I feel the fury around my heart crack, let in the vast, let in the tiny adventure of leaving the warm truck, stumbling over the rocky earth, going toward the burning tree. Under implacable midnight, my breath is a comet, illuminated by fire, a delicate plume of life.

FOOTNOTE: A controlled burn is a fire set by the Forest Service to burn off brush and understory materials that can serve as fuel for a forest fire. It is also called a "cool burn."

Stretch

In delicate mountain dusk, my landlord, John, and I shot my ancient cat. It was Saturday, the veterinarian's office was closed, and old Stretch had never known the terrifying smells in a vet's office. Dying was bad enough. And it is the western way, the country way—when death will be a gift—to mercifully kill the animal you love. To go the whole journey faithfully. Unflinching.

I stood behind my landlord, who is my friend. He asked me to keep a distance in case of ricochet. I watched his hunched shoulders, saw him bend and pet old Stretch. I put my fingers in my ears and waited.

John seemed to take forever. Not as long as it would take for Stretch, who had begun to resemble cat jerky, to die from the erosion of who-knew-how-many years and a huge abscess in his jaw. I took my fingers from my ears, knowing that I had to hear it all, see it all, taste the fear and sorrow in my mouth.

Five years ago, Stretch limped across the dirt road to my cabin after his owner abandoned him. He'd been shot even longer ago. His right paw was stiff and twisted, his heart relentlessly hungry for love, his fur short, black and white and always dusty. He'd hold up that crippled paw, stare you straight in the eye, and yowl plaintively.

"Vampire cat from hell," my pal Everett would say. And we would pick Stretch up and scratch his ears and avoid his drooly kiss. He had the underslung jaw of a pugnacious drunk and the disposition of a Buddha. He'd been an adult cat, roaming the forest and meadow, dodging stallion hoofs and pickups, when my landlord bought the cabins seventeen years ago.

I stood in the fading light. Time stretched out. John crouched. There was a pop, more like a cap gun than the sound of death. I walked up. Stretch spasmed in the green, green grass. My friend shot again, and Stretch lay still.

I petted his withered side, cupped his bony head in my hand. John put his arm around me. "It was the right thing to do. He was in terrible pain."

We stood. My friend headed back to his cabin to finish bar-
becuing steaks. I wrapped Stretch in a goofy T-shirt and carried him to the foot of my bed. That was heaven for him,
curled at my feet, holding the other cats at bay through the
night. In the morning, I would dig a hole in the red dirt and
we would bury him, in the heart of soft grass and sunshine, in
his home.

Closing

I am in the throat of the Turtle Mountain Wilderness, crouched at the base of a basalt cliff, studying a delicate braid of tracks in the sand at the bottom of the narrow wash below. I will never make it into the heart of the Turtles. I am fifty-eight, a big woman, and one of my lumbar spinal discs is flatter than it should be—too many canyon switchbacks and too much midnight city concrete, too many rapids run, too much, and never enough, boulder hopping.

The truck is parked where the roads end. If I stand up, I'll see the windshield catch the last Mojave light. Lace agate glitters and glows on the pale earth, white chalcedony roses, puddles of mineral cream. To the east, just beyond a portal that opens like a deep breath in the black rock, lies the unisex bathroom of a gang of coyotes. At the edge of a tidy deposit of scat is one scarlet flower, blossoms like bells holding light. I imagine how the flower seems to burn, as I imagine what lies west, downstream, in a streambed through which water must pour—I see the pebble curves that tell me eddies have swirled here, twice a year, once, seen only by what lives here. I would love to see that—flash floods no wider than my arm, thunder chaos of brittlebush, chalcedony, and scat.

And I am grateful to see what lies around me. Now. Here. A half-mile from the truck, a half-mile that took me an hour to cross, down into little arroyos, picking my way between firerock boulders, stopping to pick up a shard of crystal, an agate rose. I knew better than to bend over, but I did it anyway. I'll pay for it later with pain in my back. How could I not touch this lover, this fierce Mojave earth softened by winter light? How could I not, as I once lay in the perfect arms of the perfect lover who perfectly would leave, breathe in the miracle of being here, being *here*, only *now*?

The Buddhists tell us that joy lies in limitation. We Americans are taught the opposite. *More is better. Go for it all.* I move away from the cliff and look up at the ragged cobalt mountains. I want to *go* up, into the high saddle, into what leads into mystery, up where I can look out and see forever. I want more. I want it all.

My back holds me here. Some roads are closed to me forever. I consider that I have become the person whom the road-greedy claim to fight for. *But what about the handicapped? What about the elderly?*

On my slow way to this cliff, this wash, where light seems to catch on every facet of twig and stone, and shadows pour like blue lava, I walked across roads that went back to earth beneath my boots. Road Closed. Road Closed. I touched the signs. I whispered, "Yes."

I leave nothing at the base of the cliff except gratitude and make my clumsy way back to the truck. My friend, my road-buddy who loves road and roadless equally, emerges from the shadows. He is grinning. I look at his face and know I look in a mirror.

"How was it?" he asks.

"Very, very good."

"Yeah."

We walk in silence. Later, he will tell me how he traversed rock he might more prudently have avoided, and how that led him, heart in his throat, to a hidden arch in a saddle and the sight of the southern Mojave rolling in waves of mountains and desert, sunset and blue mist to the far curve of the earth. I will tell him about coyote housekeeping and bells of light and how enough is enough, and never enough. But for now, our silence is sweet earth without roads.

We camp on an abandoned mining claim. There are the requisite rusting bedspring, coils of wire, shattered Colt-45 bottles glittering like fool's agate. My friend cooks linguine with olive oil, garlic, and capers. I spread out my sleeping bag and stretch. My back throbs. Fire shoots down one leg.

"Trying to sleep is going to be a challenge," I say.

He laughs. "Would you have it any other way?"

I turn on my back, pull my legs up to my chest. Nothing releases. I look up into moonless night, Orion striding eternally young and strong across the eastern sky.

"You mean?" I ask.

"Doing it the easy way. I don't know, maybe driving up to the arch. A road."

I twist left, right, slowly. I keep my eyes open. The mountaintops that I will never see up close lie like sumi brushstrokes against the stars. I don't answer my friend. I don't have to. The way into the answer is perfectly clear.

afterknowledge

Outliving the Enemy

I write these words at least two years after the most recent essays in *Bonelight* were completed. Since that time, Flagstaff activists have closed the White Vulcan pumice mine in the sacred San Francisco Peaks; stopped a developer from putting a gated golf-course development into the Dry Lake volcanic wetland and slopes; crystallized a half-dozen powerful community organizations and challenged everything that can keep grassroots workers from working together—hubris, doubt, bickering, despair.

The New Southwest continues to be devoured. Phoenix scuttles north. Moab and Hurricane are gone. Super Wal-Mart prowls the outskirts of Flagstaff. When I call New Mexico information for Bubba's phone number ("Mile Markers"), there is no listing. I fear for places in Nevada that I will not name.

Here is a 1997 journal entry, when I was waking to the nightmare:

I can't bear the "development" going on in the forest. What an ugly, arrogant word. Perfection cannot be developed. I picture the huge houses with their multitudes of square feet, their cathedral ceilings. In the cathedrals of trees. Dishwashers, washing machines, and disposals, a bathroom per occupant, gulping water that is ebbing daily. We are a bloated people in bloated houses, starving for exactly what lives in the forests we consume.

We are bigger than we have a right to be, occupying space that is not ours. Dislocating the homes of millions, moving in, taking over. We are filthy. We foul our nests. Then we move on . . . and do it again.

What drives too many of us is a tinnitus of spirit. I know because I contain that chittering void. I read a billionaire's words: "I am insatiable for land." I wonder if he's walked every acre he owns, if he feeds ravens in winter, gathers stones, holds the trees in grateful embrace—by sunlight and moon, in every season. No wonder he's insatiable. He has the hunger of a person who bolts his meals. A person like me.

How many frantic executives decide that a second home in the pines will calm them? How many bored wives believe that a six-thousand-square-foot getaway will pump juice into a withered marriage? How many men sit across from their exhausted doctor wives and think the same? How many retired wealthy couples, their kids ungrateful and distant presences, imagine Christmas in the mountains, a cheerful family gathered under the cathedral ceiling around the antique table that Mom picked up for fifteen grand in Ouray? And, when the holiday is less than holy, take themselves to Vegas for gourmet food and oblivion?

Four years later, I continue to ask those questions. And to believe that one cannot buy peace, cannot take comfort in that which one destroys in search of peace. Or profit.

Four years later, we saboteurs continue to exist. We work with words and litigation and actions that others find unthinkable. We work by *not* doing—*not* building our "dream home," *not* entering the multiplex theater that occupies what was once eleven acres of forest, *not* spending our money in big-box chains. We are moved by passion—and by the hard blessing of being what theologian Thomas Berry calls "the nerve endings of the earth." At times, I despair at how few of us there seem to be. Other times, I know we will always be here.

Outliving the Enemy—Again

Fifteen years ago, eight of us Earth Firsters! blocked a Grand Canyon road to bring attention to a Denver corporation's plan to mine uranium thirteen miles from the South Rim. The company wanted to sink its shaft into a South Kaibab forest meadow that the Havasupai know is the belly of Mother Earth. We eight linked hands, waited to be arrested, and thought of Edward Abbey's words: outlive the enemy (so to speak) and water (so to speak) their graves. Ed is no longer alive, but the memory of his words and our arrests brought me into a loop in time.

In early June, I went on a pilgrimage into the South Kaibab— and into the past, not the old days when the Havasupai people gathered medicinal plants here near Red Butte but my own past. I walked out through knee-high sage at Red Butte, looked up at blood-orange rock weathered to the curve of an ancestral Grandmother. Sage scent carried me back those fifteen years, to a circle of Native Americans and whites praying together to stop the uranium mine. Our prayers were song, dance, and smoke from a great sage fire.

Rex Tilousi, Havasupai tribal and spiritual leader, had told us he had asked the Old Ones how best to stop the mine and heard: *prayer.* We had tried everything else—civil disobedience, challenging the Forest Service Environmental Impact Statement, watching counterappeals pile up head-high. The Havasupai risked telling sacred stories because the Forest Service had believed the testimony of a white academic who claimed, when the Havasupai, not trusting him, said little—"that they had no viable religion."

We litigated and kept faith long enough for the price of uranium to fall and the mine shaft to remain unsunk. Grateful, we drove to the site on my fiftieth birthday and played Tibetan Buddhist healing chants. The caretaker's dogs barreled out fiercely and, at the first soft thunder of the Buddhist prayers, laid down in peace.

This June, me and my pickup eleven years older, I wonder if I still knew the way. I followed power lines that were not there the first time my pals and I draped over the construction trailer a banner that read, "Hayduchess Lives!"

I drive the few miles that once seemed to my greenhorn self a long way. I spotted the mine headframe, then I was at the ten-foot barbed-wire fence, looking at the human invasion of a wildflower meadow. Much was gone: juniper, pine, the bones of Havasupai ancestors unearthed and sent somewhere. What was left was unused. Holding pond. The big metal storehouse. I thought of the second homes sitting unoccupied in western gated communities. Of waste.

The signs on the fence are faded. Energy Fuels Nuclear. Dogs on Site. I remember the prayer circles, Grand Canyon arrests, and dogs lulled by Buddhist chants. "You lose," I said to the sign and flipped what Edward Abbey referred to as the "extended digit salute."

A woman and two dogs emerged from the forest. She's the temporary caretaker, and the dogs are not the original guard-puppies who failed so sweetly at their work. I told her I was one of the people who blocked the mine. "You know," she says, "Energy Fuels Nuclear doesn't even exist anymore." She and the dogs went through the gate.

I thought of five years of work and prayer, and the belly of our Mother Earth unharmed. I thought of those of us who simply will not go away. I considered watering the grave, but the woman had turned to wave good-bye.

"Ed," I said to the shadows between the trees, "we're out-living them."

Seven weeks later, I wonder if I'll have to eat my words. Our local daily newspaper's headline is "Uranium Mine Near Canyon to Go on Line?" And the story: "President Bush's energy plan would include opening a controversial uranium mine on sacred Indian land just 15 [*sic*] miles from the Grand Canyon, but the owner of the plant says that's not so."

Matthew Putesoy, Havasupai vice chairman, says, "We oppose the mine very strongly. . . . That's our aboriginal homeland . . . we're tied to the universe from that area. They're drilling right in the abdomen of our Mother Earth."

Roy Hochstein, president and CEO of International Uranium, the mining consortium now controlling the site by virtue of the ludicrously outdated 1872 Mining Law, assures that "There's no plan to restart the Canyon Mine at this time . . . uranium prices have to improve significantly before we could consider restarting that operation."

I remember the silence at the mine site a few weeks ago, silence broken only by raven cries. I remember my words: "Ed, we're outliving them."

We have no choice but to do just that.

the black work

The Black Work

On September 11, 2001, four commercial airliners were hijacked by terrorists. Two planes were flown into the World Trade Center (WTC) Towers, one plane into a wedge of the Pentagon. The fourth plane was driven into the Pennsylvania earth as passengers fought back.

If you don't know this, it is a miracle. In the face of these huge attacks, *Bonelight* would be incomplete without the following pieces. They were written as potential National Public Radio commentaries. The first was in response to NPR's request for a one-minute piece on how I was planning to take solace, to take a little "shelter from the storm" on the weekend after the attacks. The fourth ran on KNAU, the NPR six-station public radio network serving northern Arizona.

These pieces seem to me to be part of what is called in alchemy "The Black Work"—the moment when crude material is transmuted into the divine. The substances to be changed are sealed into a retort and left till the work is complete. Now that we live in true wilderness, a place in which danger lies on all sides and GPS devices and cell phones won't help us, we have no choice but to go *in*, to the mysterious territory of our hearts. In fear. In patience, and in trust. It is my prayer that our Black Work will transform our hearts—everywhere, throughout the great neighborhood of our Earth.

SHELTER FROM THE STORM (13 SEPTEMBER 2001)

There is no longer absolute shelter. There is no "I." "We" have been linked to our global kin by this absolute loss.

And this may be a blessing, because only a privileged few, over recent decades, have been granted the illusion of permanent shelter. The rest of the human world, the earth itself, have no such assurance.

Now "we" are free to face that hard knowledge, to face into the storm—a storm that has built from the consequences of our complacency and greed, from human rage and vengeance. In so doing, we might learn to be grateful for each breath, each heartbeat, for each of our fragile connections—to each other, and to our planet.

From such gratitude springs compassion, which is, perhaps, the only permanent shelter the human heart can contain.

SILENCE (16 SEPTEMBER 2001)

I learned of the attack from my youngest son's voice on the answering machine, and I thought he was speaking of a nightmare. I turned on the radio, and in ten minutes of other voices, I learned all I needed to know. The American dream of the good old days was over. We had been propelled into new times.

I sat on my back porch in the green light of a mountain dawn. The sky just south of the airport was silent. Only wind and clouds moved above the old pine. I thought of my daughter in a big northeastern city, my sons in L.A. and Chattanooga, my son who travels weekly for business. I went to turn on the radio, and something deep within said, "No." I knew I would listen only out of fear and thus would give power to a greater fear.

I haven't watched television for years, am not on-line. It was almost easy to decide to live as though my country was a small village, to learn only what I heard directly from other peoples' lips. Later, I cheated and bought a newspaper. I took one look and fed it to the fire.

Two days later, I drove out on western roads for a book-signing and reading in Moab, Utah, then a visit with an old friend and an older compulsion in Blackhawk, Colorado. The cab of my truck was quiet. When I stopped, I listened to people. Convenience-store clerks, waitresses, the strangers who sat next to me in the jangle of casinos.

Again and again, I heard the same words from the lips of my neighbors: "A bad dream that's real. A wake-up call. Time to slow down. Time to be grateful. Time to be closer to those we love. And to know we are part of a greater family." For seconds, I felt kinship, perhaps even a little comfort.

I returned home in the difficult quiet of my own numb company, through the fierce impermanent shelter of slick-rock, mountain storms, and skies that held nothing human. I visited the most imperfect shelter of my heart and the irreducibly perfect imperfection of my past. What I found is my business. But the way I found it might be your way as well. If you want it.

The way in—and out—lay in silence. The rare, unmarketable gift of silence. For the duration of four hours, four minutes, four blessed heartbeats.

No radio. No stereo. No television. No human voices.

You can find your silence. Whether on western roads or in the heart of any city. In hunting it, you begin something new. In finding it, you are blessed. In occupying your own deep, vast quiet, you might accept a gift that will carry you away from the illusion of the good old days, and through these hard new times.

SMALL AND PETTY (27 SEPTEMBER 2001)

We admit it—between women, of course. Between me and a new friend, a feisty lady who makes her reluctantly single way through the world of the forty-something partnered and fiercely familial. I am telling her my worries about money, about book payments held up by the aftereffects of the WTC attack.

"I'm mad," I say, "and good Catholic girl that I once was, when I think about what other people lost, of course I feel disgusting."

She laughs. "Don't be so hard on yourself. I spent last night and this morning wound up in something so small and petty and wanting-a-guyish I can't believe it."

It's my turn to laugh. "What we need," I say, "is the Small and Petty Support Group."

We finish our business and I get off the phone. I remember sitting on my back porch the day my second-eldest kid was finally able to fly from Toledo to New Jersey. I was eating the excellent brie I'd bought a day before the attack, and I thought about him boarding the plane. My throat tightened. Perfect, I thought, so twenty-first-century baby-boomer American. I eat $9.99-a-pound cheese while I fear the possibility of my son's death—and the End of the World.

It's been easy to know that the greater objects of my attention before the attack—the metastatic loss of so much of our wild earth by human development; the gap between rich and poor; the corporate inhalation of little businesses, little towns, and little cultures—are still with us. I fear deeply that in our organizing, whether it is for war or peace, we will lose sight, lose memory of those hard realities.

But it may be as wise to understand that the small and petty objects of our pre-attack attention still nag us, *will* nag through our larger terrors and hopes. I think of the eighty-year-old mother of a Cockney friend and her words when I asked her how she kept going during the London bombings. "Why, one just did," she said. "And of course there were the little things. A cup of real tea. Waking up in the morning. Fussing about. You know, dear, what women do."

Fussing about. I know that after I spoke with my friend this morning and she admitted to being *only* human, I felt better. My petty fears diminished. I was able to face into the greater ones. And it occurred to me that the people of New York, the survivors and families of those lost in the attacks, might long for nothing more than the recovery of the small and petty. A spat with a beloved. The irritation of too many phone calls from a child. A day in which there are not enough hours to do all one has to do.

Perhaps it *is* time for Small and Petty Support Groups. Nothing formal. Just the safety between friends that allows us to be only human. After all, it is precisely the small and petty that make up the miracle of ordinary human life.

I fell asleep last night hoping against hope that I would wake to the voice of a latter-day Orson Welles telling the world that what we heard on our radios, saw on our televisions, was only a giant hoax, a test of what we are.

I woke this morning to know my hope had not been granted. My huge childish hope. It is time to live with the small hopes of grown-ups. I think of the people I met yesterday, on the day of the unspeakable, and of how we talked. We spoke of the world shifting. We said America now belonged to the rest of the world—to a greater family that has no guarantee of safe home-comings.

There was the young bank teller who insisted on watching for the good that would come from the horror. There was my daughter, saying she would teach a poem to her high-school students, a poem by an Armenian writer, a man spared from slaughter in the early 1900s—only by an accident of travel. There was the gas-station clerk who told me, a perfect stranger, that her boyfriend had been in Manhattan and hadn't called. Then she stepped out from behind the counter, and I wrapped my arms around her while she held me, both of us trembling, both of us beyond words.

Later, I went into the dark pine forest north of Flagstaff. There, at the base of mountains sacred to eight native tribes, beautiful to travelers from all over the world, I prayed in the only way I know. Talking to a Great Friend, then listening. In silence, I understood that vengeance can never be a moral act. It would not carry us through. I asked to know what would. And then I remembered the lovers I had seen a week earlier—before our world changed.

It was almost midnight. The couple sat at the railing above the Colorado River, on the Riverwalk between casinos in a Nevada gambling town. She was a sturdy blonde. He was a big man. She sat on a wrought-iron bench. He was in a wheel-chair. They held each other in perfect silence, her head on his shoulder, watching the huge just-waning moon rise above the ragged mountains.

I stopped in the shadows. Below the three of us, the old river caught silver and shone.

Next morning, I was seated near them in the casino coffee shop. They talked and listened with sweet intensity, their bodies leaning into their words. I saw they were in their late forties. His face was a dark moon, bloated with steroids, for who-knows-what illness.

I went to their table and asked if I could tell them something. "Of course," the woman said.

"Were you watching the moon last night?" I asked.

The man nodded. "We surely were."

"You gave me hope," I said, "of love beyond what we too often carelessly call love."

They looked at each other.

"And what," the man said gently, "do we have, if we don't have hope."